THE RAILFAN GUIDE
TO
SWITZERLAND

George H. Drury

On the cover: With the Matterhorn as a backdrop, a two-unit Gornergrat Bahn train ascends the double-track portion of the line above Riffelalp on September 18, 1990.

About the author: George Drury has been traveling by train on his own and as a group tour leader throughout North America and Europe since 1961. He has written rail travel articles for Trains Magazine, Vintage Rails, International Railway Traveler, and Rail Travel Newsletter. During his tenure as librarian of Kalmbach Publishing Co., publisher of Trains and Model Rail-roader magazines, he compiled or edited most of the books in Kalmbach's Railroad Reference Series.

All photos are by the author, except as noted in the captions.

ISBN 0-9665300-0-4

This book was prepared in May 1998, and reflects prices and schedules in effect then. Train times are from the May 1997-May 1998 edition of the Official Timetable. The hotel prices are summer rates taken from the 1996 Swiss Hotel Guide. Changes in prices, schedules, or conditions are inevitable. Hotel management can change, a waiter can have a bad day, and weather and crowds can alter the atmosphere of a place. The fares I have cited for the moun-tain-climbing railroads and the cable cars are recent but are subject to change. If you find things greatly different from the way I've described them, please let me know. — GHD

CONTENTS

An Re6/6 electric locomotive leads an express north through the Lugano-Paradiso station on September 1, 1991. This is on the line from Chiasso, on the Italian border, north to the Gotthard Tunnel, Luzern, and Zürich.

INTRODUCTION

Your travel advice must be good. You always get home.
— CHARLOTTE JOHNSTONE

THIS BOOK IS AIMED AT THE RAILFAN, the person who wants to see and experience the trains of Switzerland for their own sake, not merely as an efficient, comfortable, and pleasant way to travel to the traditional tourist attractions of the country. There's nothing wrong with such an attitude, except that you will have to explain to non-railfans why your pictures are all of trains, with mountains, glaciers, chalets, and cows as backdrop. Other railfans will understand.

Why Switzerland?

Switzerland is a good place to start an acquaintance with Europe's railroads. It is at the center of western Europe, and several north-south and east-west routes pass through the country. The Swiss rail system is compact enough to be easily understood by railfan and non-railfan alike, and if Swiss Federal Railways doesn't offer as much diversity of equipment as the German or French systems, the many private railway companies more than make up for that. So does the scenery.

You'll find many things you missed in America. The narrow gauge dining cars of the Rhaetian Railway are a fine substitute for the parlor-buffet car of the Rio Grande's San Juan. A ride on the Gotthard route or the Bern-Lötschberg-Simplon will compensate for having missed Great Northern's and Milwaukee Road's electrified crossings of the Cascades. The meter gauge RBS line between Bern and Solothurn may bring to mind the Fellsway line of the Eastern Massachusetts Street Railway. (Sorry — you won't find anything like the Illinois Terminal or Illinois landscape.) It's an easy place to be a rail enthusiast. You don't have to chase trains. They come to you.

To look at it another way, Switzer Land is a theme park for the railfan. There are trains of different sizes that go everywhere and take you to different parts of Switzer Land: Wine Land (the Rhône Valley), Cheese Land (Emmental and Gruyère), and The Real Matterhorn — and all of it looks like Heidi Land. Narrow Gauge Land begins at Landquart and Chur, and the Rhaetian Railway sometimes gives the impression of being a big model railroad — frequent trains, lots of loops and bridges and concealed track, and cars being switched in and out of trains.

Switzer Land has quaint villages, sophisticated cities, and shopping that outclasses anything you'll find in an American theme park. There are innumerable restaurants, and the train rides won't do to your lunch what amusement park rides do. The park staff are helpful and speak several languages, often including English. Switzer Land is as clean as Disneyland.

Tourism is one of the country's principal businesses, and the Swiss have been good hosts for centuries. An accompanying non-railfan can find plenty to see and do while the railfan is taking pictures of trains (and the non-railfan should read my sister-in-law's words below).

Why Drury?

In 1980 as part of a two-week trip designed to wring the maximum out of a Eurailpass I spent 24 hours in Switzerland. It wasn't long enough. In September 1983 I spent a week in Switzerland. It was the best vacation I'd ever had, but it wasn't

---

The Non-Railfan Guide to Switzerland

RAILROADS IN SWITZERLAND have nothing in common with commuter railroads in the U.S. [except the basic principles — GHD]. Trains in Switzerland are a convenient, comfortable way to see the sights without having to watch the road. With the Swiss Pass you can explore on your own. Most train windows open — lots of fresh air and you don't get blown away.

There are only a few things you should know about Swiss trains. Railroad companies own track, cars, and engines and operate trains. A few trains have names, and what that means is that the schedule has a name — the 10:57 from Chur is the Glacier Express, but the 11:57 which takes the same route and may look just the same doesn't have a name. The Glacier Express is operated by three railroads — the Rhaetian Railway from Chur to Disentis, the Furka-Oberalp from Disentis to Brig, and the Brig-Visp-Zermatt from Brig to Zermatt. Just stay in your seat and let the railroad worry about it.

Railroad track comes in several widths. Main lines and many branch lines are standard gauge. The rails are 4 feet 8½ inches apart — the same gauge that's used in North America. In mountainous areas you'll find narrow gauge track, usually with rails 1 meter apart. The only difference it makes is that standard gauge trains are bigger and can go faster.

Train schedules are posted at the stations. Departure

---

long enough. (The trip was described in the February and March 1986 issues of *Trains Magazine*, published by Kalmbach Publishing Co., P. O. Box 1612, Waukesha, WI 53187.)

In September 1986 I led a two-week tour of Switzerland for a small group of friends — a better trip than 1983. I have since led rail tours of Switzerland for the Smithsonian National Associates, Kalmbach Publishing Co., and the Society of International Railway Travelers. I have explored most of the railroading in Switzerland, and I offer my experience.

Schedules for suggested trips

The train times quoted are from the May 1997-May 1998 edition of the *Official Timetable*. Times don't change much from one issue to the next, but if you're planning a complicated day with several connections, be sure to check current schedules.

timetables are on yellow paper. Express trains are printed in red and local trains in black. First-class cars are the ones with comfortable seats. The yellow stripe over the windows helps you spot them as the train pulls in. There's also a "1" next to the door.

Swiss railways use several methods of propulsion:

• Adhesion: The wheels on the locomotive turn and the train moves, just like an automobile or a bicycle.

• Rack: Power is transmitted through a cog wheel or gear that meshes with a rack (like a ladder or a bicycle chain laid out flat) between the rails.

• Funicular: The car is clamped to a rope at track level, and the rope pulls the car up and down. Usually two cars balance each other.

• Overhead or aerial cable car: The car hangs from cables instead of running on a track, and another cable pulls the car.

In the U.S. I imagine diesel smoke of the ages permeating all railroad food. Station buffets in Switzerland are clean, bright, and in some cases nicely decorated. Their food is as good as you will find anywhere [an experienced Swiss tour guide, Felicitas Elmiger, agrees. — GHD], and the food in Switzerland is good in general. The Swiss are not into pre-packaging or microwave cooking. They don't feature Lean Cuisine. Unless you have superhuman willpower, I recommend you start your vacation lean, then eat and enjoy. — *Judith B. Drury*

The suggested itineraries start around 9:00 a.m. (0900) since you're on vacation. I have used Monday-to-Friday trains instead of weekend trains and summer schedules instead of winter schedules in the few instances where there was a difference.

I have plotted minimum-time trips, with little time between trains to eat lunch or even catch your breath. Take advantage of the hourly service on most lines and stop for lunch or to look at the view.

Notation

Switzerland has three principal languages, and Swiss Federal Railways has three names and three sets of initials: Schweizerische Bundesbahnen and SBB (German), Chemins de Fer Federaux and CFF (French), and Ferrovie Federale Svizzera and FFS (Italian). I'll use "SBB" most of the time.

Best of the best

IF I HAD a minimum of time and wanted to see the best again I'd do:

- Day 1 — Zürich to Chur, then Arosa and back.
- Day 2 — Bernina Express to Tirano and back; one way via Davos if I felt like getting up early or coming back late.
- Day 3 — Glacier Express to Andermatt, Furka-Oberalp to Göschenen, Swiss Federal (SBB) to Luzern.
- Day 4 — SBB from Luzern to Arth-Goldau, Rigi Bahnen up Mount Rigi, then down the other side to Vitznau, boat (a sidewheel steamer, I hope) to the Swiss Transport Museum in Luzern, and boat, trolley bus, or feet back to the Luzern station.

With a little more time, I'd add:

- Day 0 — Zürich to St. Gallen, ride the Trogenerbahn and the Appenzell lines, then go to Chur on Day 1.
- Day 5 — SBB meter gauge Brünig line from Luzern to Interlaken, BLS and SEZ through Spiez to Zweisimmen, MOB to Montreux, then to Zürich via Lausanne and Bern.
- Day 5a — Stop in Interlaken and ride up to Jungfraujoch, Kleine Scheidegg, Schynige Platte, or Schilthorn.
- Day 5b — The meter gauge lines at Aigle and Bex.
- Day 5c — The interurbans and suburban trolleys in the Bern-Solothurn area.

That's most of two weeks right there. Bon Voyage! Buon Viaggio! Gute Fahrt!

I use the local spellings for town and city names, because that's what you'll see when you're in Switzerland. The only cities that are much different from what you see in English are Bern and Luzern (English uses the French forms, Berne and Lucerne, but the cities are in German-speaking areas) and Genève (the French form of Geneva).

In the Italian-speaking section of Switzerland, you may see references to Zurigo and Ginevra — Zürich and Genève — and the German form of the latter is Genf. Train-indicator panels in stations apparently don't have an umlaut available — instead of ZÜRICH you'll see ZUERICH (the umlaut is a vestigial German script "e").

I use metric units because that's what my references are and that's what's used in Switzerland. The mile:kilometer ratio is about 5:8, and the conversion factors are approximately 1.6 and 0.6. For purposes of answering "Is that too far to walk?" it's 2 miles for each 3 kilometers.

The rail distances are actual kilometers, not the tariff kilometers that appear in the Swiss timetable (fares are per kilometer, and lines that are expensive to operate inflate the distance rather than use a higher rate per kilometer).

Grades are stated per mill, per thousand, a logical product of distances in kilometers and elevations in meters. To convert to percent, divide by 10.

Swiss train schedules use the 24-hour clock, so I do too. If you can't make the conversion easily, look through a discount store and you can probably find a digital watch with the 24-hour feature for less than $10.

In the schedule listings, a light underscore indicates a change of trains; a heavy underscore indicates the destination of the trip — the place to turn around and start back. After each departure time are the initials of the railway company involved and timetable references for the Swiss *Official Timetable* (S) and the *Thomas Cook European Timetable* (C).

Landquart	leave	0945	(S910, C545)
Davos Platz	arrive	1052	
Davos Platz	leave	1125	(S915, C545)
Filisur	arrive	1150	
Filisur	leave	1202	(S940, C540)
Chur	arrive	1305	

The maps will help you find the hotels, but don't try to scale distances off them.

Acknowledgments

This guide had its genesis in a guidebook I assembled in September 1986 for the friends and family who constituted that first tour group. Their comments and suggestions fleshed out the book. I thank Nancy and Jerry Angier, Judy and Hal Drury, Ron Goldfeder, and Marjorie and John Illman. I'd travel with them any time.

Advice came from J. H. Price, for many years the editor of the *Thomas Cook European Timetable*, and Max Hofmann of Swissair, associated years ago with that airline's Railroader's Tours of Switzerland. Without their help, I'd still be poring over the *Official Timetable*, wondering which trains to ride.

Felicitas Elmiger and Sandra Amstein of Bucher Travel in Luzern and Gion Rudolf Caprez of the Rhaetian Railway have given me on-the-spot guidance and extended their hospitality for many years. Ed Eisendrath, my travel agent, has cheerfully answered my questions, and I never worry about reservations he makes for me.

Readers of previous editions of this guide, in particular Klaus Matzka and Karel Peters, have provided additional information. Steve Forsyth's order for dozens of copies of this book got it out of the hand-crafted dot-matrix-printout stage. Bob Hayden has brought clarity and conciseness to the book with his editorial skill, and he has encouraged the project — that, too, is an editorial skill — since its beginning in 1986.

I thank them all.

George H. Drury
Milwaukee, Wisconsin
June 1998

SOCIAL STUDIES

Europe . . . persistently ignores the existence of Switzerland,
that most instructive patent museum of politics, apparently
only because she is a small country and people go there to see
lakes and climb mountains.
— JAMES BRYCE, THE AMERICAN COMMONWEALTH

FOR MOST PEOPLE, the mention of Switzerland conjures up a pic-
ture with the Matterhorn in the background, some gray-brown
cows grazing in the foreground, and a person in Quaint Native
Costume watching over the herd. What most people know about
Switzerland is blended from several sources: a grade-school
encounter with *Heidi* or perhaps *The Swiss Twins*, by Lucy Fitch
Perkins; a brief unit on Switzerland about the same time (third
grade, maybe); artwork on packages of cocoa and chocolate; and
The Sound of Music (and that was set in Austria, not Switzerland).
A brief review of Swiss geography, government, and history will
add depth to your train-riding experience (kind of like your ride
on Amtrak's California Zephyr is richer if you know where the
mountains are and who David Moffat was).

Geography
We'll start with the lakes and the mountains. Switzerland
covers 15,943 square miles (a little more than Massachusetts,
Connecticut, and Rhode Island) and extends 216 miles east to
west and 137 miles north to south. It comprises three regions
which run from southwest to northeast: the Jura, the Swiss
Plateau, and the Alps. The Jura is an area of steep limestone
ridges along the French border. The Swiss Plateau, despite its
name, is a hilly area extending from Lac Léman (Lake Geneva) to
the Bodensee (Lake Constance). Most of the 6.9 million inhabi-
tants (that's about two-thirds the population of southern New
England) live in the Swiss Plateau.

The Alps consist of two parallel mountain ranges. The north-
ern range includes the Bernese Alps and the Alps of Uri and
Glarus. There are only two passes through the northern range,
Grimsel Pass, between Meiringen and Gletsch, and the gorge of
the River Reuss, which is used by SBB's Gotthard route and the
Göschenen-Andermatt branch of the Furka-Oberalp Railway.
The Lötschberg and Gotthard tunnels penetrate the northern
range.

The southern range extends southwest into France and east
into Austria and Italy. Several passes cross the southern range;

the Gotthard and Simplon tunnels go through it. The two ranges are separated by the valleys of the Rhône and Rhein (Rhine) rivers. Their headwaters are separated by the Furka and Oberalp passes and the upper part of the Reuss valley at Andermatt.

Government

The official name of Switzerland is Confœderatio Helvetica — a Latin name for a country that speaks German, French, Italian, and Rhaeto-Romansh. The confederation consists of 23 cantons, three of which are divided into half-cantons (Basel-Land and Basel-Stadt, Appenzell Ausserrhoden and Appenzell Innerrhoden, and Unterwalden, divided into Obwalden and Nidwalden).

The legislature has two chambers, corresponding to the U.S. House of Representatives and Senate. The executive branch of the government is a seven-member federal council elected for four-year terms by both chambers of the legislature. The federal president is chosen from the members of the federal council and serves a one-year term.

History

Geography united the diverse peoples of Switzerland. During the 1st century B.C. the Romans conquered the Helvetii, a Celtic tribe living in the western part of present-day Switzerland. In the 5th century A.D. Helvetia was invaded by Burgundians and Alamanni (pre-French and pre-German), and in the 6th century it was absorbed by the Franks. By the 11th century Helvetia was part of the Holy Roman Empire.

In 1231 and 1240, respectively, the cantons of Uri and Schwyz, which lay along the Gotthard Pass trade route, were granted charters of independence by Frederick II. The charters released them from obligations to the Habsburgs. Frederick II was a Hohenstaufen, not a Habsburg, and the Habsburgs didn't accept those charters of independence.

Frederick's successor, Rudolf I, a Habsburg, imposed government by bailiffs. On his death in 1291, Uri, Schwyz and a third canton, Unterwalden, formed a defensive league. The anniversary of the agreement, which was signed on August 1, 1291, is a national festival.

The legend of William Tell is set in the events of that time. An Austrian bailiff named Gessler ordered the citizens of Uri to pay homage to a hat he hung in the marketplace of Altdorf. William Tell refused. Gessler forced him to shoot an apple from the head of his son. Gessler noticed a second arrow in Tell's quiver and asked about it. Tell told Gessler it was meant for him, if the first arrow missed the apple and hit the son. Gessler seized

Tell and took him away in a boat. When a storm came up, Tell took the rudder and brought the boat safely to land, then escaped and later ambushed Gessler.

Schiller's version of the legend dates from 1805. Rossini composed his opera in 1829. You know the overture. It opens with a quiet passage, heavy on the cellos. An alpine thunderstorm follows, then a pastoral episode, which has a motif for the English horn that was copied later for the horns of the Swiss postal buses. The final section is a galop (a lively dance in duple measure) — that's the part you know. It depicts either the call to arms and the rising of the Swiss patriots or the thundering hoofbeats of the Lone Ranger's horse, Silver.

Duke Leopold of Habsburg tried to put down the Swiss in 1315 and was trounced. Between 1332 and 1353 the confederation formed a series of interlocking alliances with Luzern, Zürich, Glarus, Zug, and Bern. The Habsburgs tried again to quash the Swiss, and several Swiss victories led to the Treaty of Basel in 1499. Between 1481 and 1513 the confederation added the cantons of Fribourg, Solothurn, Basel, and Schaffhausen.

About the time all that got settled, Ulrich Zwingli started preaching sermons in Zürich, kicking off the Protestant Reformation in Switzerland. The Reformation took hold in the cantons of Zürich, Schaffhausen, Appenzell, Glarus, Bern, and Basel. Luzern, Uri, Schwyz, Zug, Fribourg, and Solothurn remained Catholic. Their forces defeated the reformers and killed Zwingli.

For most of the next three centuries, Switzerland was characterized by religious conflict and political isolation. During that time Swiss forces hired out as mercenaries. The heroism of a group of those, the Swiss Guards of Louis XVI, is commemorated in the lion monument in Luzern.

By the end of the 1700s the confederation had ties with Graubünden, St. Gallen, Genève, and Neuchatel. In 1798 the French army invaded Switzerland and set up the Helvetic Republic. It wasn't a success, so Napoleon drafted a new government and created six new cantons: St. Gallen, Graubünden, Aargau, Thurgau, Ticino, and Vaud. In 1815, after the fall of Napoleon, a new constitution took effect and the confederation declared its neutrality.

The catholic cantons formed a bloc in 1834, and a brief civil war took place in 1847, followed by a new constitution in 1848. (Switzerland is now 40 percent Protestant and 46 percent Roman Catholic.) Two further measures emphasized Swiss neutrality: In 1859 mercenary service was outlawed, and in 1927 citizens were forbidden to enlist in foreign armies. Switzerland continues neutra and is not a member of the United Nations.

Et cetera

Despite Switzerland's neutrality, its military forces are very much in evidence. All males are obliged to perform military service from age 20 to age 50. During the summer you are likely to encounter troops on maneuvers. They keep their weapons and equipment at home.

The Swiss form of government emphasizes popular initiative and referendum. Several cantons still hold a kind of annual town meeting, with all the citizens assembled in the square of the capital. Women did not receive the vote nationally until 1971.

The diversity of Switzerland's culture is based on language, and that diversity prevents much in the way of a national culture. Aspiring young writers in Lausanne, to use a hypothetical example, are far more likely to study in Paris than in Zürich. Of the brief list of Swiss authors cited in the encyclopedia, I recognized only Johanna Spyri, author of *Heidi*, and Johann Wyss, author of *Swiss Family Robinson*; more recently I've become acquainted with the work of Max Frisch and Friedrich Dürrenmatt. Hermann Hesse was born in Germany but spent the second half of a long life in Switzerland.

Among Swiss artists you'll recognize the names of painter Paul Klee and sculptor Alberto Giacometti. If you ride the Rhaetian Railway, you may see prints of paintings by Giovanni Segantini on the end bulkheads of the coaches.

The best-known Swiss composer is Arthur Honegger, and his best-known work, at least among rail enthusiasts, is *Pacific 231*. Honegger and some locomotive drive wheels appear on the new 20-franc note.

Swiss scientists you have heard of include Paracelsus, who was born in Switzerland and gained much of his fame while a lecturer at the University of Basel; mathematician Leonhard Euler, who was on the old 10-franc note; and the Bernoulli family of mathematicians. It's the work of Daniel Bernoulli that keeps your transatlantic jet up in the air.

LANGUAGES

I conceive you may use any language you choose to
indulge in, without impropriety.
— W. S. GILBERT, *IOLANTHE*

YOU MAY WORRY about arriving at Zürich and not speaking a foreign language. Oh, but you do! English.

Schwyzertütsch (Schweizerdeutsch), a dialect of German, is the primary language for about 70 percent of Switzerland; French, 20 percent; and Italian, 10 percent. In a country with several official languages, people are used to dealing with other languages and making things intelligible without words. Signs often have pictographs in combination with two or more languages. You'll find that many people can speak and understand English. If you took French, German, or Italian in school, you'll be surprised how fast it comes back to you.

There are lots of foreign language instruction books. My brother and sister-in-law did well with *Just Enough German*. On their second day in Switzerland they asked for hot chocolate in a station buffet. Hal said the waitress went to the kitchen and probably had a good laugh, then brought two cups of hot chocolate.

There's a lot in those books you don't have to learn. For example, don't bother with bandages, splint, tourniquet, and ambulance. If you need any of those it will be obvious

A friend once told me all you need is "Ja," "Nein," "Ein Bier, bitte," "Noch ein Bier, bitte," and "Hilfe! Rette mich!" (yes; no; a beer, please; another beer, please; and help! save me!) I'd add "Wo ist die Toilette?" Peg Bracken says the most useful foreign-language phrases are the equivalents of "Does anyone here speak English?" "Not right now, please," and "Go away." (Spricht jemand hier Englisch? Nicht in diesem Moment, bitte. Geh weg.)

Here are travelers' glossaries arranged by the American word and restaurant glossaries in order by the German, French, and Italian. The latter include things you might not want so you can avoid them. I have included the definite articles so you can decline them properly. I have used the plural form for items you'll encounter in the plural, like strawberries and green beans.

GERMAN

Travelers' terms

arrival	die Ankunft
baggage	das Gepäck
baggage car	der Gepäckwagen
car (railroad)	der Wagen
customs	der Zoll
departure	die Abfahrt
dining car	der Speisewagen
direction (toward)	die Richtung
Do you speak English?	Sprechen Sie Englisch?
express train	der Schnellzug
first class	erste Klasse
forbidden	verboten
forward (up front)	vorn
good morning	guten Morgen
hello	Grüezi
ladies' room	die Damentoilette
late	verspätet
local train	der Regionalzug
locomotive	die Lok, die Lokomotive
men's room	die Herrentoilette
model railroad	die Modelleisenbahn
narrow gauge	schmalspur
next stop	nächste Halt
no	nein
nonsmoking car	der Nichtraucher
operation	der Betrieb
platform (station)	der Bahnsteig, der Perron
rack or cog railway	die Zahnradbahn
railcar (powered)	der Triebwagen
railway	die Eisenbahn, die Bahn
rear of the train	der Zugschluss
reserved	reserviert
reservation office	die Platzreservierung
seat	der Platz
second class	zweite Klasse
service, traffic	der Verkehr
sleeping car	der Schlafwagen
smoking car	der Raucher
station	der Bahnhof
street	die Strasse
thank you	merci vielmal, danke schön
toilet	der Abort, die Toilette

track	das Gleis
track gauge	die Spurweite
train	der Zug
train from, to	der Zug von, nach
yes	ja
you're welcome	bitte schön

Restaurant German

der Apfel	apple
bar (adj.)	cash (you'll see the word on cash-register slips)
das Bier (vom Fass)	beer (from the tap)
der Blumenkohl	cauliflower
das Brot, -brot, Brotchen	bread, sandwich, roll
das Ei, die Eier	egg, eggs
das Eis	ice cream
die Erdbeere	strawberries
der Felchen	whitefish
das Fleisch	meat
die Gabel	fork
die Gems	chamois, venison
das Gemüse, die Gemüse	vegetable, vegetables
das Glas	glass
die grüne Bohnen	green beans
heiss	hot
heisses Wasser	hot water
die Himbeere	raspberries
die Jagdspezialitäten	hunt specialties (game)
der Kaffee (koffeinfrei)	coffee (decaffeinated)
der Kaffee Hag	decaffeinated coffee (brand name)
das Kalbfleisch	veal
kalt	cold
die Karotte	carrots
die Kartoffeln	potatoes
der Käse, das Käsebrot	cheese, cheese sandwich
die Kasse	cashier's booth
der Kohl	cabbage
das Kotelett	cutlet
die Leber	liver
der Löffel	spoon
das Messer	knife
der Nachtisch	dessert
die Niere	kidneys
die Nudeln	noodles
das Obst	fruit

der Pfeffer	pepper
Pommes frites	French fried potatoes (this *is* a multi-lingual country)
das Reh	venison
das Rind, das Rindfleisch	beef
die Rippen	ribs
der Rosenkohl	Brussels sprouts
das Rösti	Swiss hash-brown potatoes
das Rückgeld	change (literally, back money)
der Saft	juice
das Salz	salt
die Scheibe	slice; open-face sandwich
der Schinken	ham
das Schinkenbrot	ham sandwich
das Schwein	pork
die Serviette	napkin
der Speck	bacon
die Speisekarte	menu
der Spiess	skewer or something on one
die Stange	draft beer (the word means "rod" and I think it refers to the handle of the tap)
die Steinpilzen	mushrooms
der Tageshit	hit of the day
das Tagesmenu	daily special meal
der Tagesteller	daily plate special
die Tasse	cup
der Tee	tea
die Teigwaren	pasta
der Teller	plate
der Toast	grilled-cheese sandwich
die Vorspeise	appetizer
warm	hot
warme Küche	hot meals (durchgehend warme Küche means available all day long)
das Wasser	water
der Wein; offener Wein	wine; open wine – available by the glass
rot, weiss	red, white
die Wurst, die Würste	sausage, sausages
die Zwiebeln	onions

FRENCH

arrivals	les arrives
baggage car	le fourgon
car (railroad)	la voiture
customs	la douane
departures	les departs
dining car	la voiture restaurant
Do you speak English?	Parlez-vous anglais?
express train	le train directe, rapide
first class	première classe
forbidden	interdit
front of the train	la tête du train
good morning, hello	bon jour
ladies' room	la toilette-dames
late	en retard
local train	le train regional
locomotive	la locomotive
luggage	le bagage
men's room	la toilette-hommes
narrow gauge	la voie etroite
next stop	prochain arrêt
no	non
nonsmoking car	le non fumeur
platform (station)	le quai
rack or cog railway	la cremaillère
railway	le chemin de fer
rear of the train	la queue du train
reserved	reservée
seat	la place
second class	deuxième classe, seconde classe
sleeping car	la voiture-lits
smoking car	le fumeur
station	la gare
street	la rue
thank you	merci
toilet	la toilette
track	la voie
track gauge	l'ecartement
train	le train
train from	le train en provenance de
train to	le train pour
yes	oui
you're welcome	il n'y a pas de quoi; je vous en prie

Restaurant French

l'assiette (du jour)	plate (daily special)
la bière (à la pression)	beer (from the tap)
le boeuf	beef
le café (sans caféine)	coffee (decaffeinated)
les carottes	carrots
la carte	menu
les champignons	mushrooms
chaud	hot
le chou	cabbage
la choucroute	sauerkraut
la cotelette	cutlet
le couteau	knife
la cuillère	spoon
l'eau	water
l'entrecôte	steak
le foie	liver
la fondue	traditional Swiss dish of melted cheese and wine to dip bread cubes into
la fourchette	fork
les fraises	strawberries
les framboises	raspberries
froid	cold
la glace	ice cream
les haricots	green beans
le jambon	ham
le jus	juice
le lard	bacon
les legumes	vegetables
le menu du jour	daily special
les nouilles	noodles
l'oeuf, les ouefs	egg, eggs
les oignons	onions
le pain, le petit pain	bread, roll
le plat du jour	plate special
le pomme	apple
les pommes de terre	potatoes
les pommes frites	French fries
la raclette	traditional Swiss dish of melted cheese served with boiled potatoes and pickled onions
les rognons	kidneys
la saucisse	sausage
la serviette	napkin

la tasse	cup
le thé	tea
la tranche	slice
la veau	veal
le verre	glass
le vin, vin ordinaire	wine, house wine
le vin rouge, vin blanc	red wine, white wine

Good things to eat

Four Swiss specialties are worth a mention. Fondue, for those of you too young to remember when a fondue pot was the perfect wedding gift (mine came from my father and stepmother, who got three), is melted cheese and wine, into which you dip cubes of crusty bread on long-handled forks. It is served with glasses of white wine, never beer. Penalties traditionally associated with losing the cube of bread in the pot mostly involve drinking more wine or kissing someone nearby.

Traditionally, raclette is melted cheese scraped from a big hunk of cheese placed near a source of heat. It is eaten with boiled potatoes and pickled onions. In restaurants it is likely to be a puddle of melted cheese with those accompaniments. In a home it is likely to be slices of cheese placed under a tabletop broiler affair, and there will be a wider variety of accompaniments.

Rösti (pronounced RER-shty) is basically hash brown potatoes. Sometimes Rösti is simply the potato that accompanies the meat, but it can also appear as a hearty and delicious main dish when it has another ingredient or two, such as bacon, cheese, sausage, onion, or egg.

Rösti often accompanies Geschnetzeltes Kalbfleisch nach Zürcher Art/Emince de Veau Zurichoise/Minced Veal Zurich Style: slivered veal sautéed along with mushrooms in butter, and finished with sour cream.

Swiss calories are all metric system, and your body absorbs only English-system calories. You'll walk them off.

ITALIAN

Travelers' terms

arrivals	arrivi
car (railroad)	carrozza
customs	dogana
departures	partenze
dining car	carrozza ristorante
Do you speak English?	Parla inglese?
express trains	treni diretti
first class	prima classe
forbidden	vietato
front of the train	testa di treno
good morning, hello	buon giorno
hotel	albergo
late	ritardo
local trains	treni regionali
locomotive	locomotiva
luggage	bagaglio
men's room	signori, uomini
narrow gauge	scartamento ridotto
next stop	prossima fermata
no	no
nonsmoker (coach)	non fumatori
platform (station)	marciapiede
rack operation	ingranaggio
rear of the train	coda di treno
seat	posto
second class	seconda classe
sleeping car	carrozza con letti
smoker (coach)	fumatori
station	stazione
thank you	grazie
toilet	toeletta, gabinetti
track	binario
track gauge	scartamento
train	treno
train from	treno da
train to	treno per
women's room	signore, donne
yes	sì
you're welcome	prego

Restaurant Italian

l'acqua	water
l'agnello	lamb
l'arancia	orange
le bibite	beverages
la birra (alla spina)	beer (from the tap)
la bistecca	beefsteak
il bue	beef
il burro	butter
calda, caldo	hot
il caffè	coffee
i carciofi	artichokes
le carote	carrots
il cavolfiore	cauliflower
i cavolini di Bruxelles	Brussels sprouts
il cavolo	cabbage
le cipolle	onions
la cotoletta, la costoletta	cutlet
il dolce	dessert
i fagiolini	green beans
il fegato	liver
le fettucine	noodles
il formaggio	cheese
fredda, freddo	cold
le frutta di mare	seafood
i funghi	mushrooms
il gelato	ice cream
l'insalata	salad
il latte	milk
il maiale	pork
la mela	apple
mista, misto	mixed
la pancetta	bacon
il pane	bread
le patate	potatoes
il pepe	pepper
la pera	pear
il pesce	fish
il pollo	chicken
i pomodori	tomatoes
il prosciutto	ham
i reni	kidney
il riso	rice
il rosbif	roast beef

il sale	salt
le salsicce	sausages
la sogliola	sole
il tè	tea
la torta	cake
la trota	trout
l'uova	egg
l'uva	grape
la verdura	vegetables
il vino (rosso, bianco)	wine (red, white)
il vitello	veal
il zucchero	sugar

Beyond spoken language

If you don't speak and understand the language, watch for nonverbal cues. I'm not sure how to describe them, but I'll give you an example from a tour a few years ago. Six of us were dining in Lugano. The food was excellent, and we did it justice. The waiter said something to Gertrude, and she smiled and said "Thank you." The waiter removed her plate — and brought back a new one with a generous second helping on it.

The tour manager, who didn't speak Italian, said he could tell from the waiter's gestures that he was not saying "If you're done with this, I'll take it away." We all helped Gertrude deal with her second helping and decided she had given the right answer after all.

TRANSLATIONS FROM THE TIMETABLE

The back cover flap of the *Official Timetable* explains most of the symbols in English (and Romansh, too). The front flap explains them in German, French, and Italian. The two therefore constitute a dictionary, sort of. A few words and phrases that occur in footnotes are worth listing.

ainsi que	also
Anschluss	connection
arrêt sur demande	stops on request
au moins	at least
battement	interval (between trains)
coincidenze	connections
correspondance	connection
Feiertage	holidays
fermata a richiesta	stop on request
fêtes	holidays
giorni feriali	work days
giorni festivi	holidays
halt auf Verlangen	stops on request
jours ouvrables	work days
keine Anschluss	no connection
mindestens	at least
ne circule pas	does not operate
nonchè	also
non circola	does not operate
ohne	except
sauf	except
salvo	except
Seite	page
si cambia	change
sowie	also
täglich	daily
Übergangszeit	connection time
umsteigen	change trains
verkehrt (nicht)	operates (not)
Werktagen	work days
die Züge warten keine Anschlüsse ab	the trains do not wait for connections

HOTEL RESERVATION LETTERS

English should work in most cases, but here are letter samples in German, French, and Italian. Spell out the month (English is okay there) — Europeans read 5/8/98 as 5 August, not May 8. Faxing your request speeds the process considerably. Or ask your travel agent to make the reservations.

English equivalent

Dear Sirs,

I plan to travel in Switzerland and would like to make a reservation in your hotel for 1 room/2 rooms for 1 person/2 persons, arriving on (date) and leaving on (date).

Please confirm if a room is available and the cost for a room with/without bath/shower and toilet.

Sincerely,

German

Sehr geehrte Herren,

Ich beabsichtige, eine Reise in die Schweiz zu unternehmen und mich in Ihrem Hotel aufzuhalten. Darf ich Sie daher bitten, 1 Zimmer/2 Zimmer für 1 Person/2 Personen vom (arrival date) bis (departure date) auf meinen Namen zu reservieren.

Ich wäre Ihnen dankbar, wenn Sie mir mitteilen könnten, ob für die gewünschten Daten noch Unterkunft verfügbar ist und was die Kosten für ein Zimmer mit/ohne Bad/Dusche und WC betragen.

Mit freundlichen Grüssen,

French

Messieurs,

J'ai l'intention de sejourner en Suisse et desirerais faire une reservation pour 1 chambre/2 chambres pour 1 personne/2 personnes. Date d'arrivée a votre hotel (arrival date). Je pense quitter votre hotel le (departure date).

Pourriez-vous m'informer de vos possibilites de logement concernant les dates ci-inclus et les prix de vos chambres avec bain/douche et WC/sans salle de bain.

Je vous prie d'agreer, messieurs, mes salutations distinguées.

Italian

Signore,

Ho intenzione di venire in Svizzera e vorrei pregarvi di reservare nel vostro albergo 1 camera/2 camere per 1 persona/2 persone dal (arrival date) al (departure date).

Favorite confermarmi se la camera/le camere e'disponibile/sono disponibili come pure il prezzo per la camera con/senza bagno/doccia/WC.

Distinti saluti,

TRIP DETAILS

PLANNING YOUR TRIP
Travel agent

A travel agent understands airline fares and schedules and has direct access to airline computers without having to hear "All our agents are busy helping other customers with their travel plans. Your call will be answered in the order in which it was received" (Translation: We don't have enough people on the payroll). Traditionally travel agents have made their money from commissions paid by airlines and hotels and have usually made no charge for their services. The airlines recently cut commissions, and many travel agents now charge a fee. The expertise and the convenience is probably worth the fee for your air ticket. You may be better off making the hotel reservations yourself by letter or fax.

Transatlantic air travel

Your choice of airline will probably depend on which frequent flier program you're in and what your nearest international gateway airport is. If you have a choice of schedules, try to arrive Zürich midmorning instead of at dawn, increasing the chance your hotel room will be ready when you arrive.

In the past I've advocated Swissair, but in recent years I've watched the service become ragged. My recent transatlantic trips on Northwest have been good. (A few years ago you'd have had to tie me up and carry me aboard to get me to fly Northwest.) Northwest's good friend KLM can get you to Zürich from Amsterdam.

When to go

Transatlantic fares have three seasons: peak, summer; shoulder, late spring and early fall; and low, November-March. On some airlines midweek travel (Monday-Thursday) costs slightly less than weekend travel (Friday-Sunday).

Early summer gives you the longest days, the best weather, and lots of other tourists. May, September, and early October are pleasant. The weather can deteriorate after mid-October. March can be surprisingly pleasant and you will probably miss rotten weather at home.

Holidays

Swiss holidays are January 1 and 2, Good Friday, Easter Monday, Ascension Day, Pentecost Monday (Whit-Monday), and December 25 and 26. Some sources also indicate January 6, August 1, and November 1. So you don't have to consult a liturgical calendar (let alone find one), here are some dates:

	1999	2000	2001	2002	2003
Good Friday	April 2	April 21	April 13	March 29	April 18
Easter	April 4	April 23	April 15	March 31	April 20
Easter Monday	April 5	April 24	April 16	April 1	April 21
Ascension Day	May 13	June 1	May 24	May 9	May 29
Pentecost Monday	May 24	June 12	June 4	May 20	June 9

Where to start and where to finish

Don't start in Zürich. Save that for the end of the trip. Choose a place an hour or so from Zürich, like St. Gallen, Luzern, or Bern. The time it takes to get there from Zürich will increase the chance your hotel room will be ready when you arrive. All three of those cities have direct trains from the Zürich airport.

If you spend your last night in Zürich, you have a 10-minute trip to the airport and most of a morning available for sightseeing or souvenir shopping. In any event, plan to spend two nights at your first stop and two nights at your last stop.

Base camp vs. moving around

Switzerland is small enough that you can cover most of it in day trips from Zürich or Bern. You trade freedom from luggage for a lack of diversity in hotels and after-dinner strolls.

There are several other ways to do a day of sightseeing free of luggage: check your luggage to your next stop; ask the hotel to hold it till midafternoon, then reclaim it and move on to the next city; or travel early in the day and check into the new hotel, assuring them that it's okay that the room isn't ready but can they hold your luggage?

Hotel reservations?

I like the security of hotel reservations, and I tend to plan my trips thoroughly. Except in the summer (and the skiing season in the ski areas) you who travel more spontaneously don't need hotel reservations, except for your first and last nights (and that's mainly for security, knowing that your first chore after arriving in Switzerland doesn't have to be finding a hotel room).

Solo vs. group travel

Some people can travel alone; others can't. I think it depends on whether you live alone and whether you speak and understand the local language. Hotels, like Noah, expect their guests to come in pairs and price their rooms accordingly.

If you are just two people with different interests, at least one of you will have to compromise. A group of four — two couples, let's say — can split up at least two ways. The men can go track down another narrow-gauge railway while the women find an art gallery; the two couples can go their own ways.

My sole small-group experience was in a group of eight: three couples and two singles, four rail enthusiasts and four not. We split into almost all possible combinations for train-riding, sightseeing, shopping, and so on. It worked fine.

A major advantage of group travel is that you have people to absorb your enthusiasm — you feel silly saying "Oh, look!" to strangers — and someone to talk with at dinner.

The package tour is an option. Be sure the theme of the tour meshes with your interests. If the emphasis of the trip is Swiss embroidery and you're going for the trains, you won't be happy.

Pass vs. tickets

The Swiss Pass is good for transportation on nearly all the railways, postal buses, city buses and streetcars, and lake boats in Switzerland. It is valid on many more railways, buses, and boats than the Eurailpass and is the obvious choice if all your travel will be within Switzerland. It is not valid for transportation on some mountain railways, but it yields a discount if you show it when you purchase a ticket.

The Eurailpass and Europass are good for international travel, but they are *not* valid on many Swiss railways, in particular the Furka-Oberalp Railway and the Brig-Visp-Zermatt Railway, traversed by the Glacier Express.

The price of the 4-day Swiss Pass is about the same as the sum of the fares for a circle from Zürich through St. Gallen, Chur, and Brig to Geneva and back to Zürich — a trip you could easily make in 4 days. If you plan to ride trains every day you are money ahead to buy a pass. Besides, you avoid having to stand in line to buy a ticket for each trip. There is a price break for two persons traveling together.

1998 Swiss Pass Prices

	First class		Second class	
	Single person	Each of two persons	Single person	Each of two persons
4 days	$264	$211	$188	$150
8 days	$316	$253	$238	$190
15 days	$368	$294	$288	$230
21 days	$403	$322	$320	$256
1 month	$508	$406	$400	$320

The Swiss Pass is available from your travel agent, Forsyth Travel Library, phone 800-FORSYTH, and Rail Europe, phone 800-4-EURAIL.

First-class seating is usually 2-and-1 and quite comfortable. Second class seats are 2-and-2, closer together, and more vertical in the back, but certainly not uncomfortable, even for trips of some distance.

Timetable and map

The *Official Timetable* consists of three volumes covering trains and boats, international trains, and buses. The domestic train and bus volumes are issued annually; the international train volume is issued twice a year.

The tables are numbered by region. The main lines are even hundreds — 100, 200, 300, etc. Table numbers for secondary lines and branches off those main lines are in those hundreds, ascending along the main lines. For example, the Lausanne-Brig route is table 100; the lines from Montreux can be found in tables 120 and 121; the three lines at Aigle are in tables 124, 125, and 126; and the routes from Martigny are in tables 132 and 133.

Table numbers for boats are generally 3000 higher than the number of the parallel or nearby rail line. Table numbers for bus routes start with the table number of the connecting rail line, then add a decimal fraction for each route.

The best map by far is the Kümmerly & Frey Swiss Railroad Map. It shows all the rail, bus, boat, and cable routes with numbers keyed to the *Official Timetable*. It does not indicate which company operates which line — for that you have to refer to the initials at the bottom of each timetable in the *Official Timetable*. Fully open, the map is almost one-fourth actual size. You can buy the Kümmerly & Frey Swiss Railroad Map at any station in Switzerland for 14.80 francs (about $10).

The *Official Timetable* is available from Rail Europe, but it is expensive. You can buy a copy at almost any railroad station in Switzerland for 16 francs. That means you'll have to use the schedules and map in this book to rough out the trip, then do the detailed day-by-day planning on the spot — and that will be mostly a matter of adjusting your schedules a few minutes one way or the other.

The *Thomas Cook European Timetable* includes all the main lines and many of the branch lines in Switzerland. It is available from Forsyth Travel Library (phone 800-FORSYTH) for $27.95 plus $4.95 for shipping.

Switzerland Tourism offices

I visited the Chicago office in January 1997 and found a help-yourself rack of leaflets and brochures, none of which was what I wanted. There was no one to ask. You might get your money's worth out of a phone call to a Switzerland Tourism

office if you have one of those dime-a-minute long-distance phone deals, or your time's worth if you are within a few blocks.
• 150 North Michigan Avenue, Chicago, IL 60601; phone 312-332-9900
• 608 Fifth Avenue, New York, NY 10020; phone 212-757-5944
• 222 North Sepulveda Boulevard, Suite 1570, El Segundo, CA 90245; phone 310-640-8900
• 154 University Avenue, Suite 610, Toronto, ON M6W 1A1; phone 416-961-3131

Guidebooks

There are lots of guidebooks. Some of them spend more time on hotels and restaurants than on things to see and do. The Baedeker guidebook and the Michelin green guide are good for sightseeing, and both have maps and an index. I prefer the Michelin guide: the maps are better and the book weighs less. The Off the Beaten Track guide to Switzerland reads well and is well illustrated.

BEFORE YOU GO

Documents

You'll need a passport. How do you get one? Ask your travel agent or check U. S. Government listings in the phone book or ask at the post office.

Your travel agent can give you a leaflet about how much of what you can bring back with you — generally speaking, $400 worth of merchandise without having to pay import duty.

Money and traveler's checks

In April 1998 the Swiss franc was worth about 66 cents. "Fr." (sometimes "SFr." or "CHF") is the abbreviation for francs, and the comma is sometimes used as the decimal point, so you'll see things like "Fr. 16,—" (16 francs) and "15,80." Coins come in denominations of 5, 2, 1, and ½ franc and 20, 10, and 5 centimes or Rappen (100 to the franc). The 2-franc piece feels like a quarter and is worth about five of them. Be sure to spend the large coins. After two or three days you will probably be able to pay for dinner with your pocket change — and you can't turn the coins in at home the way you can paper money.

It will cost you less to cash a dollar traveler's check at the bank window in Zürich Airport than to get 50 or 100 Swiss francs from your bank before you go. You can get Swiss franc traveler's checks, but I don't think they are worth bother and expense of getting them — and they are hard to cash when you get home. Don't bother with traveler's checks in denominations of less than $50.

Most large stations have change bureaus open from early morning to late evening. I understand their rates are regulated.

Visa, MasterCard, and American Express cards are widely accepted in Switzerland. Don't count on months of transatlantic float before the charges show up on your statement.

Luggage

Two pieces max. You have two hands max. The combination that works best for me is a large suitcase with wheels for the once-a-day items and a small over-the-shoulder bag for things like camera and sunglasses. Other people I've traveled with echo approval of luggage with wheels.

I haven't used a collapsible luggage cart, but it's another item to have on your mind and it requires set-up and take-down. I think suitcases with rigid handles and two wheels are more maneuverable than those with a towing strap and four wheels.

You can check your luggage from one railroad station to another for 9 francs. Swissair can send your bag from the airport where you initially check in with Swissair to any major railroad station in Switzerland. On the return trip, you can check your suitcase from most major stations to your destination airport if you are flying Swissair from Zürich or Genève. The charge for the service is 20 francs. You may have to check the suitcase the night before your departure from Switzerland.

Clothing

My feeling is that you're more likely to get through Immigration and Customs if you don't look as if you will drag down the average. To put it another way, don't dress like you would to grot out the pigsty, and I know some American railfans who do.

You might want to have a coat and tie available (or skirt, depending on your gender) if you plan to dine in a top-bracket restaurant. Other than that, men won't need anything more formal than a blazer or sport coat over an open-collar shirt, with chinos or jeans below. Women can wear slacks or jeans. Most of the skirts I saw in 1997 were on women heading for office jobs in Zürich or on elderly women, usually paired with what used to be called "sensible shoes."

Men's clothing

I take:

• A tweed sport coat or a lightweight blazer, mostly to wear over the sportshirt du jour at dinnertime.

• Water-repellent jacket and hat — easier to stow in the shoulder bag than a full-length raincoat. Unlike an umbrella, a hat leaves your hands free.

- A light folding plastic or nylon raincoat for protection against the occasional deluge.
- A sweater.
- Two or three pairs of slacks.
- One change of underwear and socks per day.
- One shirt per day-and-a-half.
- Bathrobe, slippers, pajamas — bathrobe only if I'm staying in hotels where the bathroom is down the hall; pajamas are your choice, but see the note about feather comforters on page 36.
- Two pairs of comfortable, supportive, sturdy shoes. For a long time I advocated only sturdy leather soles. Then I bought a pair of Rockport Dressports with foam-Vibram soles — they and several successor pairs have been my traveling shoes ever since.

Women's clothing

My sister-in-law's advice is to wear something on the plane you won't depend on until you have a chance to wash it. Many travel books suggest a wardrobe plan — one or two colors and everything going with everything else. This isn't bad advice for guys either, if such things matter to you.

Laundry

Some travel authorities wash things out every night, hang them up over the tub, and hope they're dry in the morning. If I'm going for no more than two weeks, I pack enough for the whole trip — doing laundry is no fun even at home. Plastic bags can segregate the dirty from the clean in the suitcase.

Other travel authorities suggest you buy cheap underwear for the trip and discard it after wearing it once. No. Buy what you usually do and leave it at home. Take all your tired, worn-out underwear and discard it as you go.

There aren't many coin-operated laundries in Switzerland. Many hotels offer one- or two-day laundry service which is grossly, exorbitantly expensive, like $113 for five days' worth (that's 1987 prices).

Weather

There are no guarantees. Europe's weather currents meet over Switzerland. You are likely to encounter morning clouds — sometimes all-day clouds — around the lakes (which means around Zürich, Luzern, and Genève). The Rhône valley is generally drier, and Zermatt is one of the driest places in Switzerland. The Engadine (St. Moritz, Samedan, Scuol) is likely to be sunny. Lugano is one of the rainiest places in Europe, and if it's not rainy, it will be hazy, unless there's a north wind that clears things out. You can get live photos of Swiss weather at http://www.topin.ch.

Cold

My theory is that you have a resistance to local germs, but the cold germs elsewhere are different. Combine that with dry air on the plane, changes of altitude, and fatigue, and chances are about even you will catch a cold. Carry along whatever soothes you when you have a cold — cough drops, tissues, tablets — like you carry an umbrella to prevent rain. (Yes, you can get those items there, but Murphy's Law applies and you'll need them when the stores are closed. Besides, the Swiss have odd cough-drop flavors.)

Home front

Most travel books are full of checklists of things to do before you leave — stop the paper, hold the mail delivery, give the key to a neighbor, put a couple of lamps on timers. Something they don't tell you to do is to have something in the cupboard or the freezer that you can have ready to eat with a minimum of effort when you get home.

You can get it there

As you head to the airport and do a mental inventory of the suitcase, it's good to remember that you can buy almost anything you've forgotten. The exception is spare parts: a second pair of glasses, for example, or whatever the breakage or loss of will inconvenience or discomfort you.

Taking off

If you can, check your baggage all the way to Zürich. If it gets lost or if it misses the connection, it is more likely to catch up with you than if it is checked only to your U.S. gateway — Boston, Chicago, or wherever. (If it's New York and you have to change airports, you can't check the bag through.) Put a change of underwear and your toothbrush and razor (or makeup) in your carry-on bag as insurance and also for freshening up in the morning.

The flight to Europe

The trip over is an all-night party: drinks, dinner, duty-free shopping, movie, 15 minutes of lights out for sleeping, breakfast, and then placing your seat backs and tray tables in their full upright and locked position and making sure that your seat belt is securely fastened in preparation for landing. (At that announcement, at least three persons will get out of their seats and go to the lavatories.)

Some authorities recommend eating lightly if at all, avoiding alcohol, and trying to sleep. On one trip I turned down the free drinks and skipped coffee with dinner, and I think I felt very slightly more alert the next day. I think it's easiest to take whatever comes and try to get a nap that first afternoon.

In the morning you may be offered a hot towel. Instead, go to the lavatory and shave or put on fresh makeup — you'll feel more like it's really morning. Fresh underwear helps, too, but it requires some contortion in the usual airplane lavatory.

NOW THAT YOU'RE THERE
Arrival

Zürich airport has two terminals, A for Swissair and a few close friends and B for other airlines. Outside the baggage claim and customs area in each terminal is an area marked with a sign that says "Treffpunkt" — the symbol is a large dot with four arrows point at it. It's a meeting point. Nearby in each terminal is a welcome desk. The range of services offered at the welcome desks includes holding tickets, passes, and information packets for pickup by incoming passengers.

Throughout the airport you'll see luggage carts. They can ride the escalators, even down to the platforms in the station.

Go through Passport Control, claim your bag, and go through Customs. You probably qualify for the "Nothing to declare" door. You'll see signs for "Railway" and "Bahn." Go down a couple of escalators through a shopping area and you're in the ticket concourse — here is where you have your Swiss Pass validated. Yellow poster timetables tell you when the next train departs for your destination and from which track. Down another set of escalators are two platforms serving four tracks. The loudspeaker will tell you which of the lettered platform sectors will have the first-class and second-class coaches (first-class cars are generally at the Zürich end of the train). If you are going beyond Zürich — to Luzern or Bern, for instance — know that the train reverses there. Sit facing backwards leaving the airport, and you'll be facing forward in 15 minutes.

Hotels

My primary criterion in listing hotels is proximity to the station. (Hotels named "Terminus," "Bahnhof," and "de la Gare" are usually near the station.) They are mostly three- and four-star hotels, but two-star hotels are just as clean and cost less. The stars denote not ambiance and luxury but such items as theratio of public space to room space and night porter's hours. The star ratings (***) shown are from the 1996 *Swiss Hotel Guide*.

Swiss hotels are different from the motels you find along the Interstate. We'll start outside and work in. Often only the reception desk is on the ground floor. A small elevator takes you up to your room. You will find it faster to come down by the stairs. If the hall is dark, look around for an illuminated switch which when pressed will give you two or three minutes of light to find your room.

Rooms are small, probably on the assumption that when you're in them you're asleep. They are shy on light, both for reading in bed and for shaving or makeup. On the bed you are likely to find a featherbed or puff instead of top sheet and blanket. In the summer and well into the fall it will be too warm. One guy I know slips it out of its giant pillowslip and uses that as a cover. Remember the puff when you pack whatever you wear to bed, and if you normally don't, you might bring pajamas for nights when the featherbed is too much.

Jet lag

Jet lag is a well-publicized malaise. It is basically a conflict between your inner clock and the clocks that run the world around you. Your plane took off at 7 p.m. and the flight took 8 hours. Your inner clock reads 3 a.m., but Zürich is bustling and the sun is high in the sky.

Your major difficulty is not jet lag but a night with no bed and probably no sleep. Check into the hotel and lie down for an hour or two, but no more than that. Then get up, have some lunch, go out and explore, eat dinner, and go to bed. (Europeans eat dinner later than many of us do — seven is probably about as early as you can get dinner.)

You won't sleep well for the first two or three nights. Your body and your mind are at least six hours out of sync, you're in an unfamiliar bed, and fresh air is available only accompanied by street noise. Someone once told me that lying down is 80 percent as good as sleeping, and after a night of horizontality you should be in good shape — or at least feel better than you did after the overnight flight.

Steve Forsyth offers a suggestion for dealing with jet lag. It condenses to: The day before you leave, load up on carbohydrates. On departure day eat nothing and drink only fruit juices, vegetable juices, and water. On the plane set your watch ahead to the new time, get comfortable, and try to sleep. When morning comes, go to the lavatory and do as many of your morning things as possible. Eat the breakfast that's offered, then after landing have a genuine breakfast and keep going all day.

Forsyth's theory is that you set your inner clock by the

In your room you may find a minibar, a small, well-stocked refrigerator. Write on the slip what you drink, and it will be added to your bill. It's semi-honor system — they ask what you've had, but they can easily check when they restock.

In the bathroom you may find sleek, stylish plumbing fixtures. You are not likely to find a washcloth, and often a packet of liquid soap-and-shampoo substitutes for a bar of soap. (It works well for washing a shirt.) Pack a washcloth and a small bar of soap. You may also find a hair dryer — the one you packed from home won't work on Swiss 220-volt electricity.

When you return from dinner and want to read or discuss plans for tomorrow, you may find a pleasant lounge that's like a

---

food and drink you put into your body: coffee and corn flakes tell your body it's 7:00 a.m.; a tuna sandwich, noon. If you eliminate these clues, the body goes on hold till it gets something definite, like coffee and a croissant.

I haven't tried his suggestions, because departure day for me usually means an early flight from Milwaukee, an airport-to-airport transfer in New York, and several hours of greeting tour members and introducing them to each other. I need food and coffee for that. It might be worth a try, though.

Other recent studies on jet lag say that exposure to sunshine helps your body adjust to the new time. I agree. My only transatlantic trip that resulted in real jet lag took off from Paris after sunset, spent 8 hours flying through the darkness, and landed at Chicago with about 8 hours of darkness to go before sunrise. For most of the next week I felt disoriented.

On the trip to Europe, give your body a subliminal message that it's morning by watching the sun rise. The flight attendant may hiss at you to put the shade down so people can sleep, but in 15 minutes she's going to turn the lights on and bring around the frozen orange juice and the pink yogurt.

On the trip home you pretty much keep up with the sun and your body, slightly bewildered, asks "You mean it's *still* 2 p.m.?" You get a meal soon after takeoff and a snack over Newfoundland. You get home at the end of the day, and your body agrees that it's the end of the day.

living room. The proprietor or some other member of the family will be tending bar, doing accounts, and answering your questions. If you stay up late, they may ask you to turn out the lights when you go to bed. Some hotels will give you two keys, and you'll find out why when you come back from a late-evening stroll. The other key is for the front door.

Breakfast is included in the room rate. It's usually coffee and rolls with butter, jam, and cheese; in the German-speaking areas you'll get sausage and maybe a boiled egg too (the egg may cost extra). On the breakfast table you'll find a cylindrical plastic container for waste paper and eggshells. Some of the little wastebaskets say something about a neat, clean table; others have sketches of roosters and hens.

You'll find sample hotel reservation letters in the section on foreign languages. The individual hotel listings include telephone and fax numbers. They begin with 41, the international dialing code for Switzerland. If you are phoning from within Switzerland, substitute a 0 for the 41.

Restaurants

We've covered breakfast. Come lunchtime, if you're used to zipping into McDonald's for a burger and fries, you'll have to change your routine. You go into a cafe (or take a table outside in the sunshine) and order from the menu. Your lunch will come with nary a piece of styrofoam in sight (unlike breakfast where practically everything seems packaged). The pre-meal basket of bread comes without butter (if you ask, they'll bring some). Take your time and enjoy lunch — you are on vacation.

There are short, incomplete menu glossaries a few pages back. They lead us to another linguistic hurdle. You ask for the menu, you get the special of the day. If you want something to read, ask for the Speisekarte or la carte. (There was one posted outside next to the door.) The menu du jour or Tagesmenu is the daily special; the assiette du jour or Tagesteller is the plate special. They are good values. You may see the word "Tageshit." Divide it between the "s" and the "h" — hit of the day.

Speaking of good value, when you order something other than the plate special the waitress or waiter may bring out your meal in serving dishes and dish up an ample portion. About the time you say, "I did pretty well by that," you'll be served another generous helping.

In restaurants you will probably have difficulty getting plain tap water with (or even without) ice. The easiest thing to do is roll with it — order a bottle of mineral water. Local draft beer is better than any standard-brand U.S. beer. The Swiss also make wine. They drink it themselves and export watches, not wine.

Dessert runs heavy to ice cream (as you will too), usually from an illustrated menu. Try the Coupe Denmark, which is vanilla ice cream and an obscene amount of chocolate sauce.

Coffee is not the staple it is at home. Except at breakfast it costs extra, several francs for a small cup. In the French-speaking area, black coffee comes in a smaller cup than cafe au lait. You can get a big cup of black coffee, but it takes perseverance.

After the coffee, ask the waitress or waiter for "l'addition, s'il vous plait," "die Rechnung, bitte," or "il conto, per favore." This is the one time during the meal you'll have a hard time catching the eye of the waitress or waiter, who is accustomed to people sitting and talking for a long time.

Service is included in meal prices, and it's usually indicated by words like "service compris" or "Bedienung inbegriffen." However, if your tab comes to something like 36.40 francs, it's customary to say, "Call it 37." Waitresses and waiters in Switzerland don't object to separate tabs around the table, even when it's two singles and three couples, not all of whom are sitting next to each other. Amazing.

Biking and hiking

You can rent bicycles at many stations. If you go walking in the fields and woods you'll find three classes of trails. A plain yellow sign indicates a Wanderweg, a walking path. Ordinary walking shoes are fine. A sign with red and white arrow point indicates a Bergweg, a mountain path, which requires hiking boots. An all-red point on the arrow means a Kletterweg, which calls for pitons, ropes, and such. The numbers on the sign are hours and minutes for an average walker in good condition.

Photographic film

Kodak film is available there — same yellow box, same film, plus a prepaid processing envelope which isn't valid in the U. S. For that reason, take more film from home than you think you might need. I've had no problem with airport X-rays fogging my film whether or not I put it in a lead-foil shielding bag.

Shopping and souvenirs

Europe is not the shopper's paradise it was decades ago. Earmark a half hour for looking through a department store and a supermarket, get out your pocket calculator, translate a few prices (which include a value-added tax) to dollars, and think kind thoughts about J. C. Penney and Safeway.

Logic says don't buy souvenirs till the last days of the trip, but if you see something you want on the second day, get it. Otherwise you'll think of nothing else for the rest of the trip. You will do better in model railroad shops, bookstores, and hardware stores than in the souvenir shops that cater to tourists. Many stores will ship items for you for a small charge. In addition, post offices sell shipping cartons.

Switzerland has 2,843,790 establishments that sell watches. At the kiosks in some stations and change bureaus in others you can get an official Swiss Railways watch with a face like the station clocks. (silver-color case with black strap, 100 francs a few years ago; gold-color case with tan strap, 150 francs). They are good-looking, reliable watches.

Airmail stamps for postcards to the U.S. cost 1.80 francs. The cards themselves are SFr .80 each. That works out to about $1.80 per postcard. You may want to rethink the necessity of sending postcards home.

Store and bank hours

Stores are generally open Monday-Saturday 0800-1200 and 1400-1800 (straight through in large cities). Banks are open Monday-Friday 0800-1200 and 1400-1630. Change bureaus in the railway stations keep longer hours.

In some cities and towns stores are closed for a half day or even a whole day each week in addition to Sunday. The sign "Ruhetag Mittwoch" (or some other day) in a restaurant window means "day of rest" — more simply, "closed." The equivalent French term is "Jour de Repose."

Swiss idiosyncrasies

Americans are far more conscious of smoking than they used to be. Europeans smoke a lot. The Swiss like to go hiking in the mountains and the fresh air, but on the train they close the windows, turn the thermostat up to "Broil," and light up. You will get some fierce looks if you open a window. Do it anyway.

The Swiss take their dogs with them. You are likely to see a dog sitting quietly under a restaurant table or in a coach. Once on a crowded Arth-Rigi Bahn train there was almost a dogfight when a second dog boarded.

As you leave the restaurant (or the hotel or the shop) you will instinctively push on the door. Pull.

Sometimes in hotels you will find, possibly quite suddenly, that the floor of the corridor is a fraction of an inch higher than the floor of your room.

City traffic is noisy, and the drivers seem aggressive, revving up through the gears and shifting badly. The mopeds are the noisest, and apparently they can go anywhere: streets, sidewalks, even station platforms. Swiss trains are quieter than ours.

It all makes good stories when you get home.

SWISS RAILWAYS

*There isn't a mountain in Switzerland now that hasn't
a ladder railroad or two up its back like suspenders.*

— MARK TWAIN

SWISS FEDERAL RAILWAYS operates 2,969 km (1,845 miles) of railroad — about half the railroad mileage in Switzerland. Swiss
Federal uses three sets of initials: SBB for Schweizerische
Bundesbahnen, CFF for Chemins de Fer Fédéraux, and FFS for
Ferrovie Federale Svizzera. The rest of Switzerland's rail mileage
belongs to approximately 70 "private" railways, some of which
are owned wholly or partly by cities or cantons.

Nationalization of Switzerland's railways was approved in
February 1898 because the railways were in financial difficulty.
Swiss Federal Railways came into being January 1, 1902. Its major
components were the "Big Five" companies: North Eastern,
Central, United Swiss, Jura-Simplon, and Gotthard.

• The North Eastern Railway (Nordost-Bahn) had lines from
Zürich south to Zug and Luzern, east through Winterthur and
Romanshorn to Rorschach, north to Schaffhausen, and northwest
to Brugg and Basel.

• The Central Railway (Central-Bahn) was centered on Olten. Its
lines reached Luzern, Rotkreuz, Brugg, Basel, Biel, Lyss, Bern,
and Thun.

• The Jura-Simplon Railway consisted of most of the lines west
of the Central, plus a Bern–Luzern route and a long line up the
Rhone valley from Lausanne to Brig.

• Smallest of the Big Five was the United Swiss Railways (Vereinigte Schweizer-Bahnen), which had a line from Wallisellen
through Rapperswil and Sargans to Chur and another from
Winterthur through St. Gallen and Rorschach to Sargans.

• The Gotthard Railway extended from Zug and Luzern south
through the Gotthard Tunnel to Chiasso on the Italian border.

The first three companies were united on January 1, 1901.
The Jura-Simplon Railway became part of SBB a year later, and
the Gotthard Railway joined SBB on May 1, 1909.

SBB's principal routes today are:

• Genève to St. Gallen via Lausanne, Bern, and Zürich. Between
Renens, just west of Lausanne, and Olten there are two parallel
routes. The through passenger route traverses hilly country
through Lausanne, Fribourg, and Bern; freight (and a lot of passenger traffic too) follows an easier route through Neuchâtel,
Biel, and Solothurn.

• Lausanne to Brig, then through the Simplon Tunnel to Domo-
dossola, Italy.
• Basel and Zürich to Arth-Goldau, then through the Gotthard
Tunnel to Chiasso. Most freight trains between Basel and
Chiasso move through Brugg and Wohlen; passenger trains go
via Olten and Luzern.
• Zürich to Sargans, Chur, and Buchs.

Another principal route, from Bern through the Lötschberg
Tunnel to Brig, is operated by a private company, the Bern-
Lötschberg-Simplon Railway.

International connections

Switzerland's principal rail connections to other countries
are at Genève (with France), Basel (France and Germany), St.
Margarethen (Austria and Germany), Buchs (Austria), and
Chiasso and Domodossola (Italy). Major gateways for interna-
tional passenger travel are Genève (to and from southern France
and Paris), Lausanne (Paris), Basel (Paris, Luxembourg, Brussels,
Frankfurt and northern Germany), Schaffhausen (Stuttgart), St.
Margarethen (Munich), and Buchs (Innsbruck and Vienna).

Initials you're likely to see on freight and passengers cars of
other countries include:

CD	Czech Republic	NSB	Norway
CFL	Luxembourg	ÖBB	Austria
DB	Germany	PKP	Poland
DR	Former East Germany	SJ	Sweden
DSB	Denmark	SNCB	Belgium
FS	Italy	SNCF	France
HZ	Croatia	SZ	Slovenia
JZ	Former Yugoslavia	SZD	Russia
MAV	Hungary	ZSR	Slovakia
NS	Netherlands		

Private Railways

The private railways come in a variety of sizes, types, and
colors much like that found in the U. S. in the 1930s and 1940s.
There are suburban lines and interurbans, short lines and main
lines, and (rare in North America) mountain-climbers. The Bern-
Lötschberg-Simplon is a main line that somehow escaped inclu-
sion in Swiss Federal Railways. The Rhaetian Railway is analo-
gous to Denver & Rio Grande Western's narrow-gauge network,
in the U. S. — but with heavy-duty electrification, hourly passenger trains, and dining cars.

All those initials

In the list below I have included a few older sets of initials
you may still see on car sides. I have included timetable refer-

ences for both the Official Timetable (numbers with S) and the Thomas Cook European Timetable (numbers with C).

Initials	Name	Tables
AB	Appenzellerbahnen	S854-856, C526, 527
AL	Aigle-Leysin	S125, C571
AOMC	Aigle-Ollon-Monthey-Champery	S126, C571
ARB	Arth-Rigi-Bahn (now Rigi Bahnen)	S602, C551
ASD	Aigle-Sepey-Diablerets	S124, C571
BAM	Bière-Apples-Morges	S156, C502
BC	Blonay-Chamby	S105
BD	Bremgarten-Dietikon	S654
BLM	Bergbahn Lauterbrunnen-Mürren	C564
BLS	Bern-Lötschberg-Simplon	S300-310, C560
BLT	Baselland Transport	S503, 505, 506
BN	Bern-Neuenberg/Berne-Neuchâtel (part of BLS)	S220, C511
BOB	Berner Oberland-Bahnen	S311, 312, C564
BRB	Brienz-Rothorn-Bahn	S475, C551
BT	Bodensee-Toggenburg-Bahn	S853, 870, C525
BTI	Biel-Täuffelen-Ins	S261
BVB	Bex-Villars-Bretaye	S127-129, C571
BVZ	Brig-Visp-Zermatt	S140, 141, C576
CEV	Chemins de fer Électriques Veveysans	S112
CJ	Chemins de fe du Jura	S236-238
CMN	Chemins de fer des Montagnes Neuchateloises	S214, 222
EBT	Emmenthal-Burgdorf-Thun	S440-443, C517
FART	Ferrovie Autolinee Regionali Ticinesi	S620, C549
FB	Forchbahn	S731
FLP	Ferrovia Lugano-Ponte Tresa	S635
FO	Furka-Oberalp	S610-612, C575
FW	Frauenfeld-Wil	S841
GBS	Gurbetal-Bern-Schwarzenburg (part of BLS)	S297, 298
GFM	Chemins de fer Fribourgeois (Gruyères-Fribourg-Morat)	S253-256, C568
GGB	Gornergratbahn	S142, C578
GN	Glion–Rochers-de-Naye (MOB)	S121, C571
JB	Jungfraubahn	S311, 312, C564
LEB	Lausanne-Echallens-Bercher	S101
LO	Lausanne-Ouchy	S103, 104
LSE	Luzern-Stans-Engelberg	S480, C552
MC	Martigny-Chatelard	S132, C572
MG	Ferrovia del Monte Generoso	S636
MGI	Montreux-Glion (MOB)	S121, C571
MO	Martigny-Orsières	S133, C573
MOB	Montreux-Oberland Bernois	S120, C566

MThB	Mittel-Thurgau-Bahn	S830, C538
MStCM	Nyon-St. Cergue-Morez	S155, C501
OC	Orbe-Chavornay	S211
OeBB	Oensingen-Balsthal Bahn	S412
PB	Pilatusbahn	S473, C551
PBr	Pont-Brassus	S201
RB	Rigi Bahnen (formerly ARB and VRB)	S602, 603, C551
RBS	Regionalverkehr Bern-Solothurn	S293-295, S420, C516
RhB	Rhätische Bahn	S910-960, C540, 541, 545-547, 575
RHB	Rorschach-Heiden-Bergbahn	S857
RhW	Bergbahn Rehineck-Walzenhausen	S858
RVO	Regionalverkehr Oberaargau	S413, 414
RVT	Chemin de fer Régional du Val-de-Travers	S221
SEZ	Simmentalbahn (Spiez-Erlenbach-Zweisimmen; part of BLS)	S320, C565
SGA	St. Gallen-Gais-Appenzell-Altstätten (now part of AB)	S854-856, C526, 527
SMB	Solothurn-Münster/Soleure-Moutier	S411
SNB	Solothurn-Niederbipp Bahn	S413
SOB	Schweizerische Südostbahn	S670-672, C525
STB	Sensetalbahn	S257
SZB	Solothurn-Zollikofen-Bern (now RBS)	S420, C516
SZU	Sihlthal-Zürich-Uetliberg-Bahn	S712, 713
TB	Togenerbahn	S859
TN	Tramway Neuchateloise	S213
TPC	Transports Publics du Chablais (AL, ASD, AOMC, and BVB)	S124-129, C571
VBW	Vereinigte Bern-Worb Bahnen (RBS)	S294, 295
VHB	Vereinigte Huttwil-Bahnen	S444, 445
VRB	Vitznau-Rigi-Bahn (now Rigi Bahnen)	S603, C551
WAB	Wengernalpbahn	S311, 312, C564
WB	Waldenburgerbahn	S502
WSB	Wynental- und Suhrentalbahn	S643, 644
YSteC	Yverdon-Ste. Croix	S212

Narrow gauge

Much of Switzerland's railway network is meter gauge. The reason for building narrow gauge lines was economy: Everything could be smaller, lighter, and less expensive than for a standard gauge railroad. Eventually it was discovered that narrow gauge railroads weren't that much cheaper. A Toyota doesn't cost much less than a full-size Chevrolet.

Nowadays the principal commodity by the narrow gauge lines is passengers. At a junction where passengers are likely to change trains anyway, track gauge doesn't matter to the passengers. Freight is a different matter. Some narrow gauge lines move standard gauge freight cars on transporters, low-slung narrow gauge cars with rails or brackets to hold standard gauge wheelsets.

The narrow gauge lines are not all short spurs off the main lines. The Rhaetian system has 375 kilometers of railroad (233 miles), most of which is electrified at 11,000 volts AC, just like the Pennsy and the New Haven used. The Rhaetian, the Furka-Oberalp, and the Brig-Visp-Zermatt form a narrow gauge system stretching across much of the width of Switzerland.

Streetcars

You'll find genuine streetcars in Zürich, Basel, Bern, and Genève. See Tables 991.35, 991.50, 992.70, and 995.95 of the bus volume of the Official Timetable. Lausanne and Neuchâtel have light-rail lines that fall somewhere between streetcars and rail-roads (tables S102 and S213). Some of the private railways resemble streetcars or interurbans in having tracks in the center of streets or alongside. The three lines at Aigle, for instance, all have stretches of street running through the town, and the Bex-Villars-Bretaye runs streetcar service between the Swiss Federal Railways station and the far end of Bex.

Steam

I've encountered steam-hauled special trains on the Bodensee-Toggenburg, the Appenzeller Bahnen, and SBB's Brünig line. Getting advance information requires a contact in Switzerland or a subscription to *Eisenbahn Amateur* (single copy, 10.50 francs from Bühler Druck AG, Postfach, CH-8027 Zürich). Posters and advertisements on station bulletin boards may provide enough information so you can see and photograph steam, considering it a kind of dividend. Don't overlook the steamboats on the lakes. They are noted in the Official Timetable.

The old Furka-Oberalp line over Furka Pass has been restored between Realp and Furka as the Dampfbahn Furka-Bergstrecke. It operates from late June to early October, mostly on weekends but daily mid-July to mid-August. The trains are powered by steam locomotives. Several trains carry buffet cars, and table 615 in the Official Timetable shows a brunch train, a moonlight fondue and raclette train, and a special photographers train. For information, telephone 41-44-6 70 42 (probably only during the operating season) or write to the Verein Furka Bergstrecke, Mitgliederdienst, Postfach 3468, CH-4002 Basel.

Several times a year the Rhätische Bahn operates trains with one of its two 2-8-0s. For information, inquire of Graubünden Tours, phone 41-81-253 31 43.

The Schinznacher Baumschulbahn operates a 3-kilometer stretch of 60-cm gauge track through a nursery ("Baumschul" is literally "tree-school"). It has five steam locomotives, including a South African Garratt. Trains run Saturdays and Sundays, 1345–1715, from the end of April to the beginning of October, except Pentecost (the day before Pentecost Monday— see page 28 — and the third Sunday in September, which is Thanksgiving or Prayer Day. A couple of years ago the fare was 5 francs. The place is about a mile from the SBB station at Schinznach Bad (the first station out of Brugg on the line to Olten and Bern, table S650). Buses from Brugg (bus table S650.30) can get you closer, as can a taxi from Brugg. For further information, write to Betriebsleitung SchBB, CH-5107 Schinznach-Dorf.

The 750-mm gauge Waldenburgerbahn operates steam occasionally. Write to Direktion, Waldenburgerbahn, CH-4437, Waldenburg, for information.

RIDING THE TRAINS

In the station

To find your train, look for the poster timetables, which list all the arrivals and departures in chronological order and give track number and destination or origin. Departure timetables are on yellow paper; the heading will be "Abfahrt," "Departs," or "Partenze," depending where you are. Fast trains are printed in red and locals in black. Arrival timetables are on white paper and are labeled "Ankunft," "Arrives," or "Arrivi."

Go to the platform for your train. You may find a board showing the composition of trains, so you can stand at the location for the car you want.

In many stations a flashing white light hanging from the platform canopy or train shed will indicate a train about to arrive (or tear through) on the adjacent track. Between the tracks you'll see a sign that reads "Überschreiten der Gleise verboten/Defense de traverser les voies/Vietato traversare i binari." Don't cross the tracks.

On the platform train indicators you may see the words "Nicht einsteigen" or "Ne montez pas." That means don't board this train. If you hear an announcement you don't understand and everyone around you suddenly starts moving to another platform, that's a good indication your train is going to be elsewhere. Follow them and ask one of your fellow passengers if you aren't sure what's happening.

The first-class portion of passenger cars is usually marked by a yellow stripe over the windows in addition to the "1" next to the door. First-class cars are generally on the front of a train going toward Zürich and at the rear of a train leaving Zürich.

Some Type IV intercity cars are equipped with seats all facing one way, like we're used to (it's called airline-style seating). The cars are marked with a symbol showing the seats. The more usual practice is for seats to be arranged in facing bays. You won't encounter many compartment cars — they are usually assigned to international trains.

You open the door by turning or pulling a handle or by pressing a button. Climb aboard and find a seat. On most trains no seats are reserved, but InterCity trains carry one first-class coach and one second marked as reserved-seat cars. Seat reservations are advised for international travel and they are required on the Glacier Express and on at least one Bernina Express.

Station stops may or may not be announced — and probably not in English. Compare your watch and the timetable, and look for signs on the platforms. Trains stop long enough so you can get off comfortably, but don't dawdle. Again you'll have to open the door yourself. You'll quickly get used to the procedure.

Eating on trains

Many mainline trains carry restaurant cars, and many more have a minibar, a little cart that comes rolling past with coffee, soft drinks, beer, wine, sandwiches, and such. A cup of mediocre instant coffee costs 3 francs. A few local trains have vending machines. The vending machines don't replace dining cars — they are a recent addition to trains that previously had no food service.

Between minibars and station buffets you're never very far from food, and both are preferable to the eating method advocated by so many other guidebooks — carrying a loaf of bread and hunks of salami and cheese in your camera bag. (However, if in your after-breakfast explorations you find a bakery that offers sandwiches and cookies, stock up. Such a lunch bought in Chur compensated for being unable to get dining car reservations on the Glacier Express.)

Bibliography

Some of these books are long out of print, but you may be able to find them in libraries.

Switzerland's Amazing Railways, by Cecil J. Allen, published in 1953 by Thomas Nelson & Sons Ltd.

Railway Holiday in Switzerland, by George Behrend, published in 1965 by David & Charles, North Pomfret, VT 05053.

Metre Gauge Railways in South and East Switzerland, by John

Marshall, published in 1974 by David & Charles, North Pomfret, VT 05053.

Schweizer Bahnen in Farbe/Des Trains et des Couleurs [Swiss Trains in Color; the text is in French and German], by M. Braun, published by Les Editions du Cabri, 06502 Menton, France.

SBB Reisezug- und Gepäckwagen/Voitures et fourgons CFF [Swiss Federal Railways Passenger and Baggage Cars], published in 1985 by Swiss Federal Railways, Bern [French and German}.

Bernina Express, by Henning Wall, distributed by Seven Hills Books, 49 Central Avenue, Cincinnati, OH 45202.

The Famous Glacier Express of Switzerland, by Hans Schweers, distributed by Seven Hills Books.

Schmalspur Paradies Schweiz [Narrow Gauge Paradise Switzerland; the text is in German], by Gustav Röhr, Hans Schweers, and Henning Wall, distributed by Seven Hills Books.

The Swiss Transportation Museum in Luzern has a selection of books in its gift shop, and you can find railroad books in ordinary bookstores. Station newsstands are a good place to find railroad magazines.

LOCOMOTIVES

Switzerland electrified its railways faster than any other nation. The country has neither coal nor oil, but it has mountains for water to flow down and spin turbines. SBB uses 15,000-volt 16⅔-hertz alternating current from overhead wires. Most of the other standard gauge railways use the same voltage. The Furka-Oberalp, the Brig-Visp-Zermatt, and most of the Rhaetian Railway use 11,000-volt alternating current. RhB's Bernina line operates on 1,000-volt DC. Most of the other narrow gauge lines use direct current, with voltages ranging from 650 to 2,500.

In January 1998 SBB's locomotive roster included 919 electric locomotives, 239 electric power cars, and 158 diesel locomotives, plus a large number of electric and diesel tractors, which are four-wheel switchers small enough that different operating rules apply. The diesel locomotives are primarily for freight and switching.

The classification system consists of a capital letter:

A	express passenger	H	rack-equipped (<u>H</u>ill)
B	mixed traffic	R	fast passenger locomotive
E	switching		or railcar (<u>R</u>apid)
G	narrow gauge (<u>G</u>auge)	T	tractor

(C and D were used for freight and slow freight)

An Re4/4^{II} is ready to depart from Interlaken Ost on September 17, 1990. The first coach is a German car.

a small letter or two:

e	electric	m	diesel
h	rack-equipped		

a pair of numbers separated by a slash:

powered axles / total axles

and sometimes a Roman numeral indicating subclass.

Most of the locomotives look alike — double enders with slope-fronted cabs. The most numerous type (273 of them) is the Re4/4^{II} (the new class is 420), 80-ton, 6320 horsepower, B-B machines built between 1964 and 1985. Looking the same but longer are the 88 members of the Re6/6 class (new class 620): B-B, 10,600 horsepower, 120 tons, 1972-1980. The Ae6/6 (new class 610) was built from 1952 to 1966 primarily for service on the Gotthard route. Nowadays they work in secondary service throughout the country. They are about the same size and weight as the Re6/6, but they have a C-C wheel arrangement and are rated at 6000 horsepower.

SBB's roster includes examples of several locomotive classes built in the 1920s and 1930s. They are held for historic purposes.

SBB has more than 130 six-wheel electric switchers, many with side-rod drive. The electric multiple-unit car is almost unknown, but SBB has lots of electric motor coaches and baggage cars capable of pulling several trailing coaches, or pushing them with the engineer in a cab coach or driving trailer.

Re 450 No. 450 001-3 stands in Zürich Hauptbahnhof on March 19, 1991, at the head of an S14 suburban train from Hinwil.

There are several new classes of locomotives. Four Re4/4[IV] locomotives, 10101-10104, were built in 1982 as experimental units with thyristor transmission. They proved unreliable and are off the roster. Since 1989 Swiss Locomotive & Machine Works of Winterthur and ASEA-Brown-Boveri of Zürich have built 119 B-B locomotives with three-phase transmission numbered in the 460 class (indicating a switch to the numbering system used by several other European railways: three digits for the class, three for the individual unit, and a check digit) and 115 B-Bs in the 450-class for pushing and pulling the new bilevel suburban trains serving the area around Zürich. The 450s are single-cab machines with a baggage compartment at the rear.

The green paint SBB has used for years on its locomotives is being replaced by red these days (the Re 450s were delivered in blue and gray, the new local-train colors). Older BLS locomotives are brown; the newest are blue. RhB, BVZ, and FO locomotives and coaches are red. SBB and RhB sell advertising space on their newest locomotives so you'll see locomotives that look like billboards for Pepsi and chocolate.

The rosters that follow are not complete and exhaustive, but they include most of the locomotives you are likely to see.

SWISS FEDERAL RAILWAYS
Locomotives

Numbers	New Class	Old Class	Wheel arrgt.	Built
10001...10050 (17)	410,411	Re4/4^I	B-B	1946-1951
11101-11349	420	Re4/4^{II}	B-B	1964-1985
11350-11370	420	Re4/4^{III}	B-B	1971
11371-11397	420	Re4/4^{II}	B-B	1981-1985
11401-11520	610	Ae6/6	C-C	1952-1966
11601...11689 (88)	620	Re6/6	B-B-B	1972-1980
450000-450114	Re 450		B-B	1989-1997
460000-460118	Re 460		B-B	1992-1996

Railcars

Numbers	Class
1051...1055 (3)	RABe EC
	Ex-Trans-Europe Express
1101-1118	RABDe12/12
	"Mirage," originally painted maroon
1401-1406	RBe4/4
1643, 1646	BDe4/4
1679	De4/4
540006-540079	RBe 540
560000-560083	RBDe 560
562000-562005	RBDe 562
550000-550004	Bem 550

Narrow Gauge (Brünig Line)

Numbers	Class	Wheel arrgt.	Built
110000-110005	De 110	B-B	1941
	Rack equipment and center truck removed		
120006-120012	Deh 120	B-2-B	1941
101961-101968	HGe 101	B-B	1990

Names

101961	Horw	101965	Lungern
101962	Hergiswil	101966	Brünig-Hasliberg
101963	Alpnach	101967	Brienz
101964	Sachseln	101968	Ringenberg

BERN-LÖTSCHBERG-SIMPLON
Locomotives

Numbers	Class	Wheel arrgt.	Built
161-195	Re4/4	B-B	1964-1983
	171 is lettered for SEZ, 179 and 180 for BN, 178 for GBS		
205	Ae6/8	1-C+C-1	1939
251, 257, 258	Ae4/4	B-B	1944
	The first high-speed electric locomotives with axle-hung motors and without guiding axles		
271-275	Ae8/8	2(B-B)	1959-1966
	Built from pairs of Ae4/4s		
465001-465005		B-B	1994-1995

Railcars

Numbers	Class	Built
721-742	RDBDe4/4	1982-1991
746-754	ABDe4/8	1954-1964
761-763	Be4/4	1953, 1956
	Some are assigned to BN, SEZ, and GBS	

FURKA OBERALP

Numbers	Class	Wheel arrgt.	Built
31-34, 36, 37	HGe4/4^I	B-B	1940, 1948, 1956
41-45	BDeh2/4	B-2	
51-55	Deh4/4^I	B-B	1972 — Smooth sides
61, 62	HGm4/4	B-B	1968
71	Gm4/4	B-B	1966
81, 82	Ge4/4^{III}	B-B	1980
	For ferry trains through the Furka Base Tunnel		
91-96	Deh4/4^{II}	B-B	1980 — Ribbed sides
101-108	HGe4/4^{II}	B-B	1985-1990

Names

51	Disentis	91	Göschenen	102	Altdorf
52	Tavetsch	92	Realp	103	Chur/Marcau da Cuera
53	Urseren	93	Oberwald	104	Furka
54	Goms	94	Fiesch	105	Alpsu/Oberalp
55	Brig	95	Andermatt	106	St. Gotthard/S. Gottardo
81	Wallis	96	Münster	107	Grimsel
82	Uri	101	Sion/Sitten	108	Nufenen/Novena

The slash indicates one name on one side of the locomotive and the other name on the other side. In September 1998 the names did not appear on 81 and 82. For a while 108 was named Channel Tunnel.

RHÄTISCHE BAHN (RHAETIAN RAILWAY)

Numbers	Class	Wheel arrgt.	Built
30	ABe4/4^I	B-B	1911 (Rebuilt 1953)
31...37 (6)	ABe4/4^I	B-B	1908 (Rebuilt 1946-1951)
	30-34 are dual voltage		
41-49	ABe4/4^{II}	B-B	1964, 1972
	1000-volt DC railcars for Bernina line		
51-56	ABe4/4^{III}	B-B	1990
	1000-volt DC railcars with three-phase		
	asynchronous motors for Bernina line		
107, 108	G4/5	2-8-0	1906
411...415 (4)	Ge6/6^I	C-C	1925-1929
	Rod-drive Crocodiles		
481-488	ABDe4/4	B-B	1957 (Rebuilt 1973)
	2400-volt DC railcars for Arosa line		
491	BDe4/4	B-B	1958
	Assigned to Bellinzona-Mesocco line		
501-504	ABe4/4	B-B	1939-1940 (R 1982-1984)
511-516	Be4/4	B-B	1971, 1979
601-610	Ge4/4^I	B-B	1947, 1953 (R 1985-1991)
611-633	Ge4/4^{II}	B-B	1973, 1984
641-649	Ge4/4^{III}	B-B	1993-1994
701-707	Ge6/6^{II}	B-B-B	1958, 1965
	Articulated bodies		
801, 802	Gem4/4	B-B	1968
	Dual power (diesel and electric)		

Names

A slash separates German and Romansh spellings; a hyphen indicates two towns sharing a station.

51–56: stations on the Bernina line (plus Hakone, Japan)

51	Poschiavo	53	Tirano	55	Diavolezza
52	Brusio	54	Hakone	56	Corviglia

601–610: mountains passes, and gorges

601	Albula	605	Silvretta	608	Madrisa
602	Bernina	606	Kesch	609	Linard
603	Badus	607	Surselva	610	Viamala
604	Calanda				

611–633: stations on the main part of the RhB plus Arosa

611	Landquart	617	Ilanz	623	Bonaduz
612	Thusis	618	Bergün/Bravuogn	624	Celerina/Schlarigna
613	Donat/Ems	619	Samedan	625	Küblis
614	Schiers	620	Zernez	626	Malans
615	Klosters	621	Felsberg	627	Reichenau/Tamins
616	Filisur	622	Arosa	628	S-chanf

629	Tiefencastel	631	Untervaz	633	Zuoz
630	Trun	632	Zizers		

641–649: other towns, some on RhB lines, some not

641	Maienfeld	644	Savogni	647	Grüsch
642	Breil/Brigels	645	Tujetsch	648	Susch
643	Vals	646	Sta. Maria/ Val Müstair	649	Lavin

701, 702: Latin names of Graubünden and Chur

701	Raetia	702	Curia

703–707: terminals on the main part of the RhB

703	St. Moritz	705	Pontresina/ Puntraschigna	706	Disentis/Mustér
704	Davos			707	Scuol

BRIG-VISP-ZERMATT

Numbers	Class	Wheel arrgt.	Built
1-5	HGe4/4^{II}	B-B	1990
11-15	HGe4/4	B-B	1929-1930
	Sloping hoods at each end of a center cab		
16	HGe4/4	B-B	1939
	Box cab; prototype of Furka Oberalp 31-37		
21-24	De4/4	B-B	1975-1976
2031, 2032	ABDeh6/6	B-B-B	1960
	Articulated railcars		
2041, 2043	ABDeh8/8	2(B-B)	1964
	Permanently coupled railcars		

Names

1	Matterhorn	21	Stalden	2041	Brig
2	Monte-Rosa	22	St. Niklaus	2042	Visp
3	Dom	23	Randa	2043	Zermatt
4	Täschhorn	24	Täsch		
5	Mount Fuji				

PASSENGER CARS

Passenger car types are:

A	first class	D	baggage	Z	postal
B	second class	R	restaurant		

The passenger car and locomotive classifications can be combined, yielding something like "ABDeh4/4" for an electric motor car with first and second class seating, a baggage compartment, and apparatus for rack operation.

There are two general types of passenger cars. Cars for international service and the green-and-gray Type IV cars are built to the standard UIC design (Union International des Chemins de fer): 26.4 meters over buffers and a deep arched roof.

For domestic service SBB uses a standard lightweight car that is lower and somewhat shorter than the UIC car. There are several classes of these. The oldest, built from 1937 to 1957, have disappeared. They had doors at the one-third points of the car, double-width doors, or center doors. The Type I cars, built from 1956 to 1967, have doors near the ends. The Type II cars, built from 1965 to 1974, can be distinguished by windows that don't come up so close to the eaves and by small windows between the door and the end of the car. Type III cars, built between 1972 and 1975, are red and light gray and have tapered bodies, narrower at the eaves than at the floor. They were SBB's first air-conditioned cars. They were intended to have tilting mechanisms installed. They are now assigned to push-pull trains. Double-deck coaches operate on suburban push-pull trains around Zürich.

SBB's traditional dark green paint is being replaced by dark blue and gray for local and suburban service, dark green and very light gray for intercity service, black, blue, and green for regional trains, and two-tone gray for international service. Some refurbished cars are still dark green but with a narrow turquoise stripe.

It may occur to you that the railcars of many of the private lines look alike, except for paint. That's because they are products of only two or three builders. Remove the paint from North American locomotives and you'll find the same sort of resemblance.

SIGNALS

SBB has begun to install a new signal system, with a white circle around three lenses grouped in a triangle for home signals; for distant signals, a white square around the lenses. Both home and distant signals can have a number in lights to indicate speed in tens of kilometers per hour that applies.

OLD SYSTEM

Home signal	Indication	Preceding distant signal
R	Stop	Y Y
G	Proceed	G / G
G / Y	Diverging clear (40 km/h)	Y / G
G / G	Diverging clear (65 km/h)	Y G / G
G / G / G	Diverging clear (95 km/h)	G / G Y

(Diverging signal speeds are for SBB; other companies may specify lower speeds, such as 30 and 45 km/h on RhB.)

NEW SYSTEM

Home signal	Indication	Preceding distant signal
R	Stop	Y
G	Proceed at track speed	G
G / 9	Proceed at 90 km/h	Y / 9
Y / 4	Proceed at 40 km/h; stop at next signal	Y / 4

A sign with an upward-pointing chevron means track speed applies after the train has passed the sign. A yellow light with an illuminated chevron underneath lets a train enter an occupied station track prepared to stop.

SIGNALS USED IN STATIONS

Starting/brake-test signal

(usually found at engineer's eye level)

W	Apply brakes	W W / W	Brakes okay
W / W	Release brakes	W / G	Start

Ground-level signals

(similar to Pennsylvania Railroad practice)

W W	Stop
W / W	Caution
W / W	Proceed

Switching signals

(usually rows of white lights)
— Stop for trains and switching moves
+ Stop for switching moves
× Switching crew finish up and get out of the way

On RhB's Arosa and Bernina lines, the + means the opposing signal is cleared for an oncoming train; a vertical row of lights means the turnout is lined and locked for the track the signal governs.

SIGNS AND SYMBOLS

 Beginning of rack   End of rack

 (Yellow, on the corners of passenger cars) Doors close automatically when the train starts.

 123 per mill upgrade for 456 meters (similarly downgrade for a sign with a downward-pointing arrow)

CITIES AND REGIONS

BASEL

Basel (Bâle in French), the second largest city in Switzerland, is in the northwest corner of the country where the borders of France, Germany, and Switzerland meet. It is at the upper limit of navigation on the Rhein and is a major port and commercial center. The Swiss, German, and French rail systems connect at Basel. German intercity trains arrive and depart at the east end of the SBB station; French trains use a special section at the west end. In the portion of the city on the right bank of the Rhein is the Badischer Bahnhof, where German local trains terminate. Access to the platforms involves border formalities.

HOTELS

Basel is about an hour from Zürich, Solothurn, and Luzern, so you can make it an easy day trip without having to pack up and move. Baedeker, Fodor, and the Swiss Hotel Guide list several hotels near the SBB station. I have not stayed in any of these (nor even overnight in Basel), but I think you can trust Swiss hotels. Let me know what you think if you stay in any of these.

• Schweizerhof (****), Centralbahnplatz 1, CH-4002 Basel, phone 41-61-271 28 33, fax 271 29 19. Single with bath, 150-250 francs; double with bath, 210-350 francs.

• Victoria am Bahnhof (****), Centralbahnplatz 3-4, CH-4002 Basel, phone 41-61-271 55 66, fax 271 55 01. Single with bath, 140-220 francs; double with bath, 190-300 francs.

• St. Gotthard (****), Centralbahnstrasse 13, CH-4002 Basel, phone 41-61-271 52 50, fax 271 52 14. Single with bath, 165-220 francs; double with bath, 220-320 francs.

• Helvetia (***), Küchengasse 13, CH-4051 Basel, phone 41-61-272 06 88, fax 272 06 22. Single with bath, 115-160 francs; double with bath, 165-290 francs.

• Bristol (**), Centralbahnstrasse 15, CH-4051 Basel, phone 41-61-271 38 22, fax 271 38 45. Single without bath, 75-95 francs; double with bath, 150-200 francs; double without bath, 110-140 francs. A reader reports that the Bristol's restaurant is excellent.

• The Hotel Terminus in Brugg, about 40 minutes toward Zürich by fast train, is also a good base for exploring the Basel area. It is described in the section on Zürich.

STREETCARS

Basel has a streetcar system, Baseler Verkehrsbetriebe (BVB), but probably of greater interest is Baselland Transport (BLT), a meter-gauge suburban system formed in 1974 from the Birseckbahn (BEB), the Birsigthalbahn (BTB), the Basellandschaftliche Ueberlandbahn (BUeB), and the Trambahn Basel-Aesch (TBA). BLT cars are yellow with red stripes and run into Basel on BVB tracks (BVB cars are green).

BLT line 10 (table 505) is considered the longest streetcar line in Europe (25.6 kilometers, 15.9 miles, 62 minutes running time end to end). It was created in 1986, when the lines to Dornach and Rodersdorf were combined. The Dornach end of the line parallels SBB's route to Delémont (table S230). Connections can be made at Dornach and Münchenstein. Leymen, the next-to-last stop on the line to Rodersdorf, is in France. There is a restaurant in the station at Rodersdorf.

BLT line 11, the former Trambahn Basel-Aesch (about 8 kilometers long), and line 14 to Pratteln are shown in table S991.35 (the bus volume of the Swiss timetable). Rush-hour line 17 (table S506) appears to be a short-turn service on the Rodersdorf end of line 10 combined with through running on BVB to Basel Wiesenplatz east of the river.

WALDENBURGERBAHN

Not far from Basel is the 750-mm gauge Waldenburgerbahn, Switzerland's only railway of that gauge. You can ride out and back or continue by postal bus to the Oensingen-Balsthal Bahn, from which you can return directly through Olten or continue to Solothurn and return via Delémont. Neither the Waldenburgerbahn nor the Oensingen–Balsthal Bahn appears in the Thomas Cook European Timetable.

Basel	leave	1030	1053	SBB (S500)
Liestal	arrive	1045	1102	
Liestal	leave	1105		WB (S502)
Waldenburg	arrive	1128		
Waldenburg	leave	1148		bus (table 412.20)
Balsthal	arrive	1213		
Balsthal	leave	1218	1246	OeBB (S412)
Oensingen	arrive	1227	1255	
Oensingen	leave	1233		SBB (S410)
Olten	arrive	1250		
Olten	leave	1305		SBB (S500)
Basel	arrive	1349		

Oensingen	leave	1259	SBB (S410)
Solothurn	arrive	1311	
Solothurn	leave	1315	SMB (S411)
Moutier	arrive	1345	
Moutier	leave	1349	SBB (S230)
Basel	arrive	1438	

Liestal to Waldenburg

Distance: 13 km
Company: Waldenburgerbahn (WB)
Maximum grade: 38 per mill

The line climbs, and the rate of climb increases as the trip progresses. WB runs steam occasionally — see page 46.

Waldenburg to Balsthal

Bus service is at least hourly, but most of the schedules are footnoted for weekdays, workdays, weekends, and/or Sundays only. Many trips involve a layover or a change at Langenbruck, about halfway along the journey.

Balsthal to Oensingen

Distance: 4 km
Company: Oensingen-Balsthal Bahn
Maximum grade: 12 per mill

The OeBB is short and flat, but there is interesting equipment on the property, such as the ex-German Federal Railway three-unit electric trainset it uses in passenger service.

OTHER INTERESTING RAIL OPERATIONS NEAR BASEL

At Rheinfelden, between Basel and Brugg (table S700), the Feldschlösschen brewery sends much of its output to SBB rails behind its own steam locomotives. Last time I went past I saw a steam locomotive and antique coaches parked at the station.

At Mulhouse, France, a half-hour train ride from Basel, is the French Railway Museum. It has its own rail station, but train service is infrequent — I'm told the bus isn't much better.

Between Waldshut, Germany, and Koblenz, Switzerland, Deutsche Bahn (German Railway) operates an hourly railbus across the Rhein on a long bridge (table S702). Koblenz is on the line from Winterthur through Bülach to Baden (table S701).

The line from Winterthur to Schaffhausen (table S762) crosses the Rhein just above a major waterfall. From April through October trains stop at Schloss Laufen am Rheinfall, which is a short walk from the falls. Across the river is a year-round stop at Neuhausen. Trolley buses 1 and 9 from the Schaffhausen station can put you within walking distance of the right (west) bank of the river.

BERN

Bern (Berne in French) is the capital of the Swiss Confederation and the location of Swiss Federal Railways' headquarters. It is a rich city for the tourist with lots of things to see, and its setting in the center of a sharp bend in the Aare River is a scenic one. Non-railfan sights are the arcaded streets — it's a good city for shopping — the clock tower, where all kinds of figures come out and parade around and hit bells every hour on the hour, and the bear pit at the apex of the bend of the river. (The emblem of the city is a bear.) If any children with you have been acting up, show them the statue of the ogre eating children.

For the railfan there's a pedestrian overpass at the north end of the station with good views. A few blocks farther is a four-track concrete arch bridge over the river, with a parallel street bridge offering good photo opportunities in the morning. Schanzenstrasse offers good views of the west end of the station. (The station is on a curve.) The city has streetcars — some of the narrowest you'll see, and there are some new low-floor cars.

HOTELS

• Krebs (∗∗∗), Genfergasse 8, CH-3011 Bern, phone 41-31-311 49 42, fax 311 10 35. Single with bath, 120-140 francs; single without bath, 80-100 francs; double with bath, 145-195 francs; double without bath 140-153 francs.

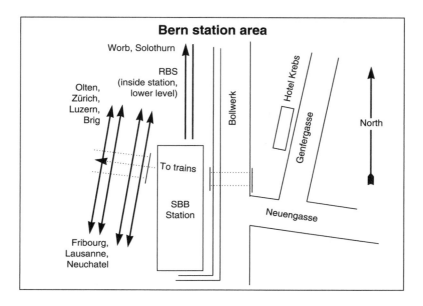

Bern station area

North of Bern Hauptbahnhof SBB crosses the River Aare on a concrete arch bridge. A local train made up of older cars rolls north across the bridge on October 1, 1986.

Come out of the station not to the south into the plaza where the streetcars are but to the east, passing under the street named Bollwerk and up the escalator to Neuengasse. Follow Neuengasse away from the station for a short block, then turn left on Genfergasse. Ask for a room away from the street if you're staying over a weekend — the area is populated with noisy young people, and the window provides the only ventilation.

Friends recommend the Hotels Bären and Bristol, in Schauplatzgasse: After you come through the passage under the tracks, turn to the right and walk south through the shopping area, then up to Bubenbergplatz. Running directly to your left is Spitalgasse, with streetcar tracks in it. Beyond it heading off diagonally is Schauplatzgasse.

• Bären (****), Schauplatzgasse 4, CH-3011 Bern, phone 41-31-311 33 67, fax 311 69 83. Single with bath, 135-170 francs; double with bath, 195-240 francs.

• Bristol (****), Schauplatzgasse 10, CH-3011 Bern, phone 41-31-311 01 01, fax 311 94 79. Single with bath, 135-170 francs; double with bath, 195-240 francs. The Bären and the Bristol are Best Western Swiss Hotels under the same management.

RAILWAY COMPANIES IN ADDITION TO SBB

Bern-Lötschberg-Simplon (BLS)
Gurbetal-Bern-Schwarzenburg (GBS)
Berne-Neuchatel/Bern-Neuenburg (BN)
Regionalverkehr Bern-Solothurn (RBS) — meter gauge
    GBS and BN are both part of the BLS system. RBS includes the former Vereinigte Bern-Worb Bahnen (VBW) and the Solothurn-Zollikofen-Bern (SZB)

RECOMMENDED TRIPS

Burgdorf, Huttwill, and Solothurn
Jungfraujoch (see the section on Interlaken)
Thun
Worb Dorf

BURGDORF, HUTTWILL, AND SOLOTHURN

This circle includes standard gauge trains, a meter gauge interurban, and a meter gauge suburban line. Also shown is a longer loop south from Burgdorf to Langnau and Wolhusen

Bern	leave	0850	0859	SBB (S450, C500)
Burgdorf	arrive	0904	0921	
Burgdorf	leave	0911	0924	EBT (S441, S444)
Langnau	arrive	I	0952	
Langnau	leave	I	1000	SBB (S460, C515))
Wolhusen	arrive	I	1030	
Wolhusen	leave	I	1032	VHB (S445)
Huttwil	arrive	0955	1058	
Huttwil	leave	1007	1107	VHB (S441)
Langenthal	arrive	1028	1128	
Langenthal	leave	1035	1135	RVO (S413)
Solothurn	arrive	1126	1226	SNB (S413)
Solothurn	leave	1133	1233	RBS (S420, C516))
Bern	arrive	1210	1310	

Bern to Burgdorf

Distance: 23 km
Company: SBB
Maximum grade: 12 per mill
    The 0850 is a semi-fast train from the Genève airport to the Zürich airport; the 0859 is a Bern-Olten local. At Burgdorf, go through the subway to the westbound platform.

Burgdorf to Ramsei and Langnau

Distance: 21 km
Company: Emmental-Burgdorf-Thun (EBT)
Maximum grade: 12 per mill

Your train will probably be on one of the stub tracks west of the station. At Oberburg, 5 minutes out of Burgdorf, you'll pass EBT's engine house. The line ascends gently from Burgdorf through Ramsei to Langnau.

The Emmental-Burgdorf-Thun was formed in 1942 by the merger of the Emmentalbahn and the Burgdorf-Thun Bahn. The latter was electrified in 1899 with a three-phase system; it was converted to a 15,000-volt AC system in 1932 and 1933.

The EBT is under the same management as the Solothun-Münster Bahn (Soleure-Moutier in French) and the Vereinigte Huttwil-Bahnen. It is associated with the Oensingen-Balsthal Bahn (OeBB), the Sursee-Triengen, and the Sihlthal-Zürich-Uetliberg-Bahn (SZU). EBT's cars are now labeled "Regional-verkehr Mittelland" and "Transports Regionaux du Mittelland."

Langnau to Wolhusen

Distance: 37 km
Company: SBB
Maximum grade: 20 per mill ascending, 23 per mill descending
The 1000 train from Langnau leaves Bern for Luzern at 0930, if you want to shortcut part of the EBT. From Langnau the SBB line climbs for 15 km to a summit (853 meters) at Escholzmatt, then descends at 22 and 23 per mill to Wolhusen.

Wolhusen to Huttwil

Distance: 25 km
Company: Emmental-Burgdorf-Thun (EBT)
Maximum grade: 25 per mill
The line climbs out of Wolhusen, descends, then climbs again to a summit just south of Hutwill. The scenery is agricultural. You may see a steam engine stored at Huttwil.

Ramsei to Huttwil

Distance: 19 km
Company: Vereinigte Huttwil-Bahnen (VHB)
Maximum grade: 25 per mill
The 0911 from Burgdorf goes to Huttwil, diverging from the Burgdorf-Langnau line at Ramsei, 12 km from Burgdorf, and running through agricultural country. The line crosses a summit between Sumiswald-Grünen and Affoltern-Weier. Until 1994 the train ran as a mixed train from Ramsei to Huttwil.

Huttwil to Langenthal

Distance: 14 km
Company: Vereinigte Huttwil-Bahnen (VHB)
Maximum grade: 21 per mill (descending)
The ride from Huttwil to Langenthal follows a small river, and the scenery isn't especially exciting.

Langenthal to Niederbipp

Distance: 11 km
Company: Regionalverkehr Oberaargau (RVO)
Track gauge: 1 meter
Maximum grade: 65 per mill

Niederbipp to Solothurn

Distance: 14 km
Company: Solothurn-Niederbipp (SNB)
Track gauge: 1 meter
Maximum grade: 45 per mill

Regionalverkehr Oberaargau (formerly Oberaargau-Jura Bahnen), the Solothurn-Niederbipp Bahn, and the Biel-Täuffeln-Ins are under the same management. RVO and SNB pool their equipment. The SNB line has a third running rail from Niederbipp to Oberbipp for handling standard-gauge cars.

OJB and SNB are interurban lines, and they give you an idea of what interurban travel in the U.S. used to be like. The cars offer only one class of seating. The end platforms are spacious, apparently for baggage and overflow passengers, and there seems to be no objection to passengers riding there.

Just out of Langenthal a branch diverges to run northeast, then east, then south to St. Urban (named for the patron saint of city transit), a bit over 6 kilometers. There is a large abbey at St. Urban. At Mumenthal, a request stop, the line crosses over the SBB route between Bern and Olten on a road bridge. It looks like a good photo spot, with long shots in both directions.

The Langenthal–Niederbipp line descends to cross the Aare River at Aarwangen, then climbs out of the valley for the run to Niederbipp, where it ducks under SBB's Solothurn–Olten line and runs into a stub-end station where the trains reverse.

From Niederbipp to Solothurn the profile is up hill and down dale. The line ends in the Solothurn station plaza after a short stretch of street running.

Solothurn to Bern

Distance: 34 km
Company: Regionalverkehr Bern-Solothurn (RBS)
Track gauge: 1 meter
Maximum grade: 45 per mill

RBS operates an intense suburban service from Bern to Worb over two routes, and from Bern to Solothurn. The line enters Bern's main station via a 1.2-km subway constructed in 1965.

A streetcar line between Zollikofen and Bern opened in 1912, and a connecting railway began service between Zollikofen and Bern in 1916. The two companies merged in 1922 as the

Solothurn-Zollikofen-Bern and built a new route around Zolli-kofen to bypass restrictive clearances. Similar clearance problems prompted the construction of a new line into Bern in 1965.

The 0659 trip from Solothurn and the 1713 departure from Bern offer buffet service. The latter might make a nice pre-dinner ride. Any suburban trolley that provides food service deserves your business.

THUN

Expresses on the SBB main line will get you from Bern to Thun in 20 minutes (tables S292, S300, and C560). Consider instead the Gürbetal-Bern-Schwarzenburg trains in table S298 (GBS is part of the Bern-Lötschberg-Simplon system) and the EBT trains in tables S442, S440, and C515.

Bern	leave	0821		GBS (S298)
Thun	arrive	0908		
Thun	leave	0924		EBT (S440, C517)
Konolfingen	arrive	0938		
Konolfingen	leave		0958	SBB (S460, C515)
Bern	arrive		1019	
Konolfingen	leave	0939		EBT (S442, C517)
Burgdorf	arrive	1008		
Burgdorf	leave		1043	SBB (S450, C500)
Bern	arrive		1106	
Burgdorf	leave	1014		EBT (S400, C517)
Solothurn	arrive	1041		
Solothurn	leave		1103	RBS (S420, C516))
Bern	arrive		1140	

Bern to Thun

Distance: 34 km
Company: Gürbetal-Bern-Schwarzenburg (GBS)
Maximum grade: 25 per mill

The first part of the ride from Bern is suburban but the scenery becomes rural, and there are views of the mountains ahead and to the left. The line offers a look at the Bern airport. O'Hare it ain't.

Thun has a busy station if you want to sit and watch trains. Above the town is a castle that is open May–October. It offers a good view of the mountains to the west and south.

Thun to Solothurn via Konolfingen and Burgdorf

Distance: 62 km
Company: Vereinigte Huttwil-Bahnen (VHB)
Maximum grade: 25 per mill

EBT operates twice hourly over most parts of this route.

Through trains connect Thun and Solothurn every two hours; other trains require a change of trains at Burgdorf and possibly Hasle-Rüegsau.

The EBT train climbs at about 2 percent through agricultural country to Konolfingen (15 km from Thun), where it crosses SBB's Bern–Luzern line (tables S460 and C515). You can change here for a quick ride into Bern; the line from Luzern joins SBB's line from Thun about halfway to Bern.

The EBT train continues north, climbing more steeply (2.5 per cent), passing through two tunnels before reaching the summit north of Grosshöchstetten. The train descends to Burgdorf (41 km from Thun), passing EBT's shops at Oberburg just before reaching Burgdorf. The train reverses at Burgdorf, then continues to Solothurn, descending gently across a plain.

You'll have a 35-minute wait if you return to Bern from Burgdorf, but you'll see several trains during that time.

WORB DORF
Distance: 25 km
Company: Regionalverkehr Bern-Solothurn (RBS)
Maximum grade: 39 per mill

For a good ride that takes a bit over an hour, ride RBS Line W from the lower level of BernHauptbahnhof to Worb Dorf. Trains run every 15 minutes and make the 15-kilometer trip in 24 minutes (table S294).

Then return to Bern on line G. Trains run every 10 or 20 minutes, and the 10-kilometer trip takes 24 minutes (table S295). Line G crosses SBB's Bern–Thun line at Gümligen. You can stop there to watch trains and take pictures. Just north of Gümligen, Line G takes to the middle of a street and eventually winds up running on streetcar tracks to the center of Bern.

The Bern-Muri-Gümligen-Worb Bahn began operation in 1898. In 1907 its title was shortened to Bern-Worb Bahn. It was electrified in 1910.

The Worblentalbahn was chartered in 1911, and in 1913 opened a more easterly route from Worb to a connection with the Bern-Zollikofen Bahn at Worblaufen. The Worblentalbahn and the Bern-Worb Bahn merged in 1927 to form the Vereinigte Worb Bahnen (United Worb Railways), and that company united with the SZB in 1984 to form Regionalverkehr Bern-Solothurn (Bern-Solothurn Regional Transit). In passenger count RBS is Switzerland's largest private railway.

BRIG

Brig (Brigue in French) is at the north end of the Simplon Tunnel. Two principal rail routes join here, SBB's route up the Rhône Valley from Lausanne and the Bern-Lötschberg-Simplon line from Bern. Just beyond the Simplon Tunnel is Domodossola, Italy, where Swiss Federal Railways meets Italian State Railways.

In the plaza in front of the SBB-BLS station in Brig are meter gauge tracks used by the Furka-Oberalp and the Brig-Visp-Zermatt. The station buffet has tables and chairs right on the platform at track 1, and there are plenty of trains to see.

Brig is a commercial town rather than a tourist center, but it has a castle that is worth a visit. It's perhaps a ten-minute walk from the station and the Hotel Victoria.

Another touristy, non-railroady thing to do is to ride the postal bus over Simplon Pass to Iselle or Domodossola, Italy.

HOTELS

• Victoria (∗∗∗), Bahnhofstrasse 2, CH-3900 Brig, phone 41-28-23 15 03, fax 24 21 69. Single with bath, 105-130 francs; double with bath, 160-200 francs. The Victoria is right across the plaza from the station. It has been refurbished recently, and its dining room is good.

• Readers of this guide have recommended the Hotel Londres (∗∗∗) at Bahnhofstrasse 17, a couple of blocks up from the station. Phone 41-28-23 82 33; fax 23 26 21. Single with bath, 85-110 francs; double with bath, 120-160 francs.

• Hotel Touring (∗∗∗), CH-3930 Visp; phone 41-28-46 47 77, fax 46 47 97. Single with bath, 72-90 francs; double with bath, 122-153 francs. Visp (Viège in French) is 7 minutes (SBB main line) or

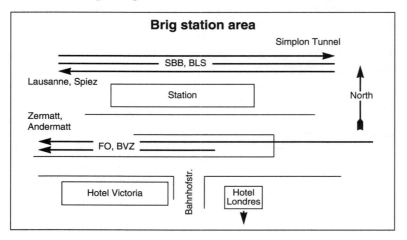

Brig station area

Simplon Tunnel

SBB, BLS

Lausanne, Spiez

Station

North

Zermatt, Andermatt

FO, BVZ

Hotel Victoria

Bahnhofstr.

Hotel Londres

11 minutes (BVZ) west of Brig. In 1994 my tour group was rerouted there because of flood damage in Brig. The Hotel Touring proved quite good. Rooms on the track side of the hotel offer a view of the east end of the Visp station platforms and a long-distance look up at the BLS line to the Lötschberg Tunnel, and the BVZ track runs right next to the building — easier train-watching than in Brig. The hotel, which is at the east end of the station plaza, doesn't have a restaurant for lunch and dinner, but the station restaurant serves excellent food.

RAILWAY COMPANIES IN ADDITION TO SBB:
Bern-Lötschberg-Simplon (BLS)
Brig-Visp-Zermatt (BVZ) — meter gauge
Furka-Oberalp (FO) — meter gauge

RECOMMENDED TRIPS
Andermatt, Locarno, and Domodossola
Furka Steam Railway
Goppenstein
Iselle and Domodossola by bus
Montreux, Zweisimmen, and Spiez
Riederalp and Bettmeralp
Zermatt and Gornergrat

ANDERMATT, LOCARNO, AND DOMODOSSOLA
Clockwise
Brig	leave	0907	FO (S610, C575)
Andermatt	arrive	1046	
Andermatt	leave	1050	FO (S612, C577)
Göschenen	arrive	1105	
Göschenen	leave	1150	SBB (S600, C550)
Bellinzona	arrive	1254	
Bellinzona	leave	1307	SBB (S630, C548)
Locarno	arrive	1330	
Locarno	leave	1520	FART (S620, C549)
Domodossola	arrive	1700	SSIF
Domodossola	leave	1713	SBB (S100.3, C590)
Brig	arrive	1747	

Counterclockwise
Brig	leave	0900	SBB (S100.3, C590)
Domodossola	arrive	0932	
Domodossola	leave	0945	SSIF (S620, C549
Locarno	arrive	1125	FART
Locarno	leave	1330	SBB (S630, C548))

Bellinzona	arrive	1353	
Bellinzona	leave	1406	SBB (S600, C550)
Göschenen	arrive	1508	
Göschenen	leave	1511	FO (S612, C577
Andermatt	arrive	1522	
Andermatt	leave	1531	FO (S610, C575)
Brig	arrive	1734	

The Brig–Andermatt route is covered in the section on the Glacier Express (page 92); the Andermatt–Göschenen–Bellinzona route is covered in the section on the Gotthard Route (page 94).

Bellinzona to Locarno

Distance: 21 km
Company: SBB
Maximum grade: 13 per mill (descending)

The main line of the Gotthard Railway originally followed the east shore of Lago Maggiore; that line is now considered a branch. (It was the last SBB route to be electrified, except for a freight-only line near Schaffhausen.) The Bellinzona-Locarno line branches from the Gotthard main line at Giubiasco, follows the old main route to Cadenazzo, then branches off to Locarno, lowest station in Switzerland.

Beneath the SBB station is the station of the Ferrovie Autolinee Regionali Ticinesi, the railway "rejoicing in the name of FART," to quote George Behrend in *Railway Holiday in Switzerland*. In Locarno its line runs through a new tunnel, less picturesque than the former street trackage but easier for operation.

Locarno to Camedo

Distance: 20 km
Company: Ferrovie Autolinee Regionali Ticinesi (FART)
Maximum grade: 60 per mill
Track gauge: 1 meter

Camedo to Domodossola

Distance: 32 km
Company: Societa Subalpine di Imprese Ferrovie (SSIF)
Track gauge: 1 meter

The line from Locarno to Domodossola is the Centovalli Railway, which may indeed cross 100 valleys. It has more than 50 major bridges and more than 30 tunnels. Work began in 1913 and took 10 years to complete because of World War I and the collapse of the bank that was financing the line. FART was formed in 1961 by the amalgamation of several rail, bus, and tram lines in the Locarno area.

Marshall's book says that to see the woods west of Re in their autumn colors with snow-covered peaks beyond is an unforgettable experience. Others have described the line as an electrified Durango-Silverton line. What do you suppose Julie Andrews could do with "Domodossola" and "Re"?

The line terminates in a subway underneath the platforms of the SBB-FS (Ferrovie dello Stato, Italian State Railways) station at Domodossola, Italy.

Domodossola to Brig

Distance: 41 km
Company: SBB
Maximum grade: 25 per mill

Until a tunnel in Japan eclipsed it, the Simplon Tunnel was the longest in the world — and it is actually two tunnels, each 12 miles and some long. Work began in 1898. Unexpected high temperatures and underground water sources, hot and cold, set the work back, and the first tunnel entered service in 1906. The pilot tunnel was then enlarged to hold a second track; it opened in 1921. As in the Gotthard Tunnel, about midway through is a pair of crossovers to allow trains to switch tracks.

Between Domodossola and the south portal of the tunnel is a spiral tunnel, hard to appreciate because it is entirely underground. There is a brief flash of daylight at Iselle di Trasquera, then it's dark for 12 miles to Brig.

FURKA STEAM RAILWAY

The Furka Steam Railway operates Friday, Saturday, and Sunday only mid-June to the beginning of October, plus limited service Monday through Thursday mid-July to mid-August.

Brig	leave	0829	0907	FO (S610, C575)
Realp FO	arrive	0957	1030	request stop
Realp DFB	leave	1010	1125	DFB (S615)
Furka	arrive	1100	1215	
Furka	leave	1125	1300	
Realp DFB	arrive	1203	1338	
Realp FO	leave	1300	1354	
Brig	arrive	1451	1551	

The 0907 from Brig operates mid-June to mid-September.

Realp to Furka

Distance: 7 km
Company: Dampfbahn Furka Bergstrecke (DFB)
Maximum grade: 110 per mill

When the Furka Base Tunnel was opened in 1982 the old line over Furka Pass was abandoned. In recent years track has been restored to the east slope of the pass, from Realp to the summit, then down to the east portal of the old Furka Tunnel. Some of

Engine No. 2 of the Dampfbahn Furka Bergstrecke, a 2-6-0T, takes water on October 5, 1997.

the steam locomotives that were sold to Viet Nam when the Furka Oberalp Railway electrified have been brought back and restored to service, painted dark blue and lined in gold.

The DFB station at Realp is perhaps a 10-minute walk west of the Furka Oberalp station. The DFB train climbs quickly above the treeline, and the scenery in the pass looks like pictures you've seen of trains in the Andes. At the end of the line the engine cuts off and runs around the train. Refreshments are available there.

GOPPENSTEIN

Brig	leave	0914	0958	BLS (S300, C560)
Goppenstein	arrive	0940	1021	
Goppenstein	leave	1039	1044	
Brig	arrive	1103	1110	

Distance: 25 km
Company: Bern-Lötschberg-Simplon (BLS)
Maximum grade: 27 per mill

The ride from Brig up to Goppenstein and back is the most spectacular portion of the Bern-Lötschberg-Simplon main line (see the description below). Expresses leave Brig at 58 past each hour and Goppenstein at 39 past each hour. Local trains depart Brig at 14 or 48 past and return from Goppenstein at 44 past, for the most part. Some local trains are operated with motor cars and trailers, with vestibules right behind the engineer's cab so you can look out the front.

A hiking trail follows the south ramp between Brig and Goppenstein; the best part is between Hohtenn and Eggerberg, both served by Brig–Goppenstein local trains and by postal buses from Gampel-Steg and Visp, respectively. The Hohtenn–Eggerberg walk takes about 5 hours. Of the stations along the south ramp, Ausserberg looks like it offers the best train-watching and train-photographing possibilities. It is served by Brig–Goppenstein local trains and postal buses from Visp. Even in the stations remember that the trains come fast and quietly and usually keep to the left.

ISELLE AND DOMODOSSOLA BY BUS

Brig	leave	0915	bus (S145.40 — bus timetable)
Iselle	arrive	1038	
Domodossola	arrive	1105	
Domodossola	leave	1200	
Iselle	leave	1227	
Brig	arrive	1350	

Buses depart from the east end of the station plaza in Brig. In winter they go only to Gondo, just short of the border, or Iselle, at the south portal of the Simplon Tunnel. In summer a few buses continue to Domodossola.

Two cautions if you go to Iselle: Only a few trains stop there, so plan to ride the bus both ways or carefully check the train service in table S100.3. The timetable says southbound buses stop at the Iselle station but northbound buses stop on the main road. Trains run frequently between Domodossola and Brig; from Domodossola you can also ride east to Locarno.

MONTREUX, ZWEISIMMEN, AND SPIEZ

Brig	leave	0918	SBB (S100, C570)
Montreux	arrive	1033	
Montreux	leave	1100	MOB (S120, C566)
Zweisimmen	arrive	1258	
Zweisimmen	leave	1305	SEZ (S320, C565)
Spiez	arrive	1351	
Spiez	leave	1358	BLS (S300, C560)
Brig	arrive	1503	

Brig to Montreux

Distance: 121 km
Company: SBB
Maximum grade: 18 per mill

The Rhône valley trends west and southwest from Brig to Martigny, where it turns 90 degrees to the northwest. As you would expect, the line down the Rhône valley from Brig has an easy grade — for the most part about 10 per mill with a few stretches up to 14 or 15 per mill. For about 10 kilometers between Leuk and Sierre/Siders the grade is steeper, as much as 18 per mill (descending westbound), and there is a 5-kilometer stretch of single track. Along the south side of the valley at that point is the remains of a prehistoric rockslide. I would expect that the rockslide, the step in the valley, and the boundary between the German- and French-speaking areas are all connected, but I'll leave a discussion of that to the linguistic geologists.

The Montreux-Spiez route is discussed on page 128.

Spiez to Brig

Distance: 74 km
Company: Bern-Lötschberg-Simplon (BLS)
Maximum grade: 27 per mill

The BLS began by taking over the Spiez-Frutigen Railway in 1907 as part of a scheme to build a transalpine main line south from Bern to Brig to avoid a long detour through Lausanne and Martigny. Construction of the Lötschberg Tunnel began in 1906, before railway lines reached up to either end of the tunnel. In 1908 workers encountered a fissure that was full of water, and it was several months before work could be resumed, with the tunnel diverging considerably to the east of its proposed alignment. The 9 mile, 140 yard tunnel was completed in 1913. It is double track throughout, and the lines leading to it have been double-tracked in recent years.

From Spiez the line ascends the valley in a series of steps, passes through the Lötschberg Tunnel, follows a gorge south, then emerges into the Rhone Valley about 1500 feet above the valley floor. It takes about 12 miles to descend to Brig, and the angle is about the same as a DC-3 would do it. It is one of the most spectacular pieces of railroad engineering in Switzerland.

The connections at Zweisimmen and Spiez are tight, but service is hourly, so take time to eat or sit and watch trains.

The Bern-Lötschberg-Simplon recently opened a path along part of the north ramp of the Lötschberg line. The entire path runs from Kandersteg to Frutigen and takes about five hours; the meat of it lies between Kirche Kandergrund and Blausee-Mitholz, where the two horseshoe curves are. It takes about an hour to walk between the two.

Only one or two trains in each direction make local stops, so you'll need to use bus from either Frutigen or Kandersteg to reach the ends of the path at Blausee-Mitholz (the Balmhorn bus stop) and Kandergrund (the Altels bus stop). BLS operates the bus; it is shown in table S301 of the rail volume of the *Official Timetable* and 301.10 of the bus volume. A brochure about the path is available at the Kandersteg and Frutigen stations for 10 francs (this *is* Switzerland). There are a number of information signs along the path too.

In places the path is right next to the track ("hautnah" in the magazine article where I saw it — skin-close) and the trains are quiet, so stay alert. Remember that the trains usually keep to the left. A friend advises that there is some steep climbing involved — this trek is not for the faint of heart.

RIEDERALP AND BETTMERALP

Brig	leave	0915	FO (S610, C575)
Mörel	arrive	0926	
Betten FO	arrive	0933	
Betten FO	leave	1215	
Mörel	leave	1221	
Brig	arrive	1234	

If you feel down at the bottom of things in Brig, here is a remedy. At Mörel and Betten FO (the station for the village of Betten way up on the side of the valley) aerial cable cars run up to the villages of Riederalp (tables S2330 and S2331) and Bettmeralp (table S2337). The cable cars run frequently, and trains run more or less hourly.

From both those villages other cable cars or chair lifts can take you higher. If you look west from Bettmeralp, you'll see the Matterhorn on the skyline.

ZERMATT AND GORNERGRAT

Brig	leave	0918	BVZ (S140, C576)
Visp	leave	0929	
Zermatt	arrive	1042	
Zermatt	leave	1112	GGB (S142, C578)
Gornergrat	arrive	1155	
Gornergrat	leave	1219	
Zermatt	arrive	1303	
Zermatt	leave	1415	
Visp	arrive	1530	
Brig	arrive	1542	

Zermatt and the Matterhorn rate a day, but Zermatt is not a place you go for train-watching. It's a tourist center, probably the most touristy place in Switzerland. It's accessible only from Brig and Visp (connections are better at Brig). See page 142.

CHUR

Chur (Coire in French, Cuera in Italian, Curia Rhaetorum to the Romans) is one of the oldest towns in Switzerland. It is compact enough for exploring on foot. Liechtenstein is nearby; the easiest way to get there is to take the train to Sargans or Buchs and the postal bus from there (table S880.95).

Chur is the gateway to the canton of Graubunden (Grisons in French, Grigioni in Italian). The Rhaetian Railway (Rhätische Bahn, RhB) is the principal railway system in this corner of the country — SBB's penetration is limited to the line from Sargans to Chur. The new bus station above the west end of the Chur station platforms is worth a look.

HOTELS

• ABC-Terminus (✶✶✶✶), Ottostrasse 8, CH-7000 Chur, phone 41-81-252 60 33, fax 252 55 24. Single with bath, 150-200 francs; double with bath, 210-290 francs. Cross the tracks of RhB's Arosa line in the plaza in front of the station, turn left, and follow the street that faces the tracks a block. The hotel is opposite the freight transfer yard; only the reception desk is at the street level. I have stayed at the ABC-Terminus several times and found it

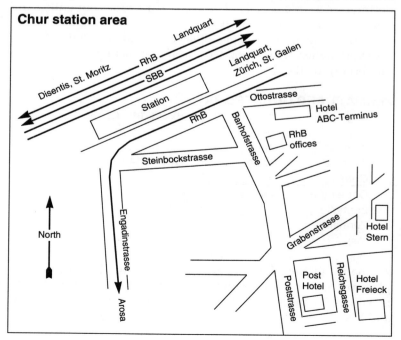

Chur station area

clean, comfortable, convenient, and, better than any of that, friendly. The hotel was extensively rebuilt in 1990 and 1991.

• Post Hotel (***), Poststrasse 11. Phone 41-81-252 68 44, fax 252 01 95. Single with bath, 90-120 francs; without bath, 75-85 francs; double with bath, 150-200 francs; without bath, 130-150 francs. Walk up Bahnhofstrasse, and continue across Grabenstrasse on Poststrasse. The entrance is next to a clothing store, and you'll have to look for it. Only the reception desk is at street level. The rooms are comfortable, and the staff is pleasant.

• Romantik Hotel Stern (***), Reichsgasse 11, CH-7000 Chur. Phone 41-81-252 35 55, fax 252 19 15. Single with bath, 105-140 francs; double with bath 195-260 francs. Walk up Bahnhofstrasse past the Rhaetian Railway general office building and the art museum, turn left on Grabenstrasse and cross it, and at the end of the block you'll be facing the Hotel Stern across Reichsgasse. Look for a star on the sign. The Stern has received high marks from members of my tour groups.

• Hotel Freieck (***), Reichsgasse 44/50, CH-7002 Chur. Phone 41-81-252 17 92, fax 253 34 19. Single with bath, 90-110 francs; without bath, 75-85 francs; double with bath 150-200 francs. Just beyond the Post Hotel turn left and you'll be heading straight for the side of the Freieck. Turn right, then left to reach the entrance.

• Hotel Drei Könige (**), Reichsgasse 18, CH-7002 Chur. Phone 41-81-252 17 25, fax 252 17 26. Single with bath, 95-140 francs; without bath, 75-85 francs; double with bath 140-180 francs; without bath, 110-130 francs. Head for the Hotel Stern and turn right on Reichsgasse.

I've eaten well in Chur. I can recommend the restaurants of the Hotel Freieck and the Hotel Stern, the Cafe Controversa just around the corner from the Stern, the Rätushof Cafe on Bahnhofstrasse just above Steinbockstrasse, an Italian restaurant called The Obelisk, the Marsöl Restaurant in the upper part of town, and the Churerhof restaurant, on the Plessur River.

Readers of this guide highly recommend the Hotel Adler in Reichenau-Tamins, 11 minutes west of Chur, where the Rhaetian Railway splits to go to St. Moritz and Disentis. The hotel is a few minutes' walk from the station — start by crossing the river on the bridge behind the station. Friends who live nearby seconded their recommendation of the restaurant and took me to dinner there one evening. Excellent!

• Hotel Adler (***) CH-7015 Reichenau. Phone 41-81-37 10 44, fax 37 24 96. Single with bath, 80 francs; double with bath, 140 francs.

Sargans, on the way from Zürich and St. Gallen to Chur,

might be a convenient place to stay. Readers have recommended the Zum Ritterhof. It is close to the station, and rooms with a view of the tracks are available.

• Hotel zum Ritterhof (***), CH-7320 Sargans; phone 41-85-723 77 77, fax 723 77 79. Single with bath, 65-85 francs; double with bath, 98-120 francs.

RAILWAY COMPANIES IN ADDITION TO SBB

Rhätische Bahn (RhB) — meter gauge

RECOMMENDED TRIPS

Arosa
Brig and Zermatt (Glacier Express)
Davos and Filisur
St. Moritz
Tirano, Italy, via Bernina Pass

AROSA

Chur	leave	0900	1250	RhB (S930, C541)
Langwies	arrive	0940	1333	
Arosa	arrive	0958	1358	
Arosa	leave	1000	1500	
Langwies	leave	1017	1517	
Chur	arrive	1102	1602	

The 0900 is an exception to the hour-interval service on the line to Arosa. Most Arosa trains leave Chur at 50 past the hour.

Distance: 26 km
Company: Rhätische Bahn (RhB)
Maximum grade: 60 per mill

Arosa became a popular resort because of its setting, but the carriage road from Chur had to detour at great heights above the Plessur River. A railroad was first proposed about 1890, but not until 1911 was the Chur-Arosa Railway established. The line was opened at the end of 1914, and it was operated electrically from the beginning.

From its starting point in the plaza in front of the SBB-RhB station the line follows streets as far as the carbarn. A tunnel and a subterranean station for the Arosa line were proposed a few years ago; stating in print that I've seen no evidence of construction will bring out the bulldozers and earthmovers.

Arosa is at about the same elevation as St. Moritz. RhB does that climb in 89 kilometers and Arosa in only 26. The line follows the right bank of the Plessur, gradually climbing above it. Sit on the right leaving Chur for the best views. The major engineering work on the line is the Langwies Viaduct, which was the longest reinforced concrete span in the world when it was opened in 1914 (287 meters total, 96 meters for the main span, 62 meters above the river). Second longest was the Grundjetobel Viaduct, just north of Langwies. It is more difficult to see, because the train approaches it straight on in both directions.

What to do in Arosa? There's not much of railfan interest, so have lunch, walk around the lake, or perhaps take a cable car up to the Weisshorn (table S2910).

The Chur-Arosa Railway became part of the RhB in 1942. The line was electrified at 2000 volts DC, and over the years the voltage was increased to 2400. In 1997 it was converted to the 11,000-volt AC system used on most of the rest of the RhB.

Shortly after the electrification was converted RhB rebuilt several cars for the Arosa Express. The blue-painted train includes a first-class car with wide windows and a bar car. It is assigned to the 1000 and 1450 departures from Chur and the 1300 and 1700 trips from Arosa.

Langwies is worth an hour stopover coming or going, or if time is short going just that far. Opposite the station the railway has thoughtfully placed benches for a good view of the viaduct. (Photographers: It will be backlit except possibly just before sundown in late June. Good luck.)

BRIG AND ZERMATT

This is the Glacier Express — or rather, these are. One train each way runs year round. Two or three others are summer only. If you can't get reservations on the Glacier Express, remember that numerous local trains cover the route, offering the same scenery without the surcharge but with changes of train at Disentis and Andermatt. The Glacier Expresses do not carry checked baggage — it moves on local trains or goes the long way around. For schedules and a full description of the Glacier Express turn to page 89.

DAVOS AND FILISUR

Chur	leave	0854	RhB (S910)
Landquart	arrive	0912	
Landquart	leave	0945	(S910, C545)
Davos Platz	arrive	1052	
Davos Platz	leave	1125	(S915, C545)
Filisur	arrive	1150	
Filisur	leave	1202	(S940, C540)
Chur	arrive	1305	

| Filisur | leave | 1200 | (S940, C540) |
| St. Moritz | arrive | 1253 | |

Landquart to Filisur

Distance: 69 km
Company: RhB (meter gauge)
Maximum grade: 35 per mill

A standard-gauge railroad was opened along the valley of the Rhein from Lake Constance through Sargans to Chur in 1856. In 1858 a railroad was proposed south to the spa town of Davos, but another 30 years passed before the Landquart-Davos Narrow Gauge Railway was incorporated. The 50-kilometer line was opened in 1890 to Davos from a point where the Landquart River flows into the Rhein a few miles north of Chur. The gravelly land there was not good for farming but was the logical place for the new railroad's shops and a company town.

The line to Davos crosses the river plain, then begins climbing, at 35 per mill for the most part to Küblis, then at 42 per mill. Klosters used to be a stub-end reversing station. The old bridge that trains used leaving Klosters for Davos is now a footbridge.

The train continues in the same direction and enters a concrete bridge-tunnel affair leading to a tunnel. Diverging to the left at that point is the new line leading to the Vereina Tunnel, under construction from a point south of Klosters to the lower Engadine (the valley of the Inn River northeast of S-chanf).

The train burrows into a tunnel leaving Klosters and emerges on the hillside headed northwest. It turns again, climbing at 45 per mill, and you can get a glimpse of the north portal of the Vereina Tunnel below. After another pair of hairpin turns, the train crosses a summit (1625 meters) at Davos Wolfgang, then descends into the central part of Davos. Most trains on the line terminate at Davos Platz. The station buffet there is decorated in a railroad theme, with photographs of such exotic trains as the Hiawatha and the Empire State Express.

Five kilometers short of Filisur is the Wiesen Viaduct. Get off the train at Wiesen, cross the tracks east of the station, and follow the footpath west along the tracks. The best photo location is at the west end of the viaduct. Walk across the viaduct on the walkway cantilevered out from the south side of the bridge. If, as I did, you look down through the ⅛-inch gaps between the planks, you will probably find yourself clutching the railing, turning around, and going back to solid ground. However, the view from the far end is good. Keep looking ahead, not down. Think of me when you get to the spot where you can feel my fingerprints etched into the railing.

Filisur

• Hotel Rätia, Bahnhofstrasse, CH-7477 Filisur. Phone 41-81-72 11 05, fax 72 23 53. Single with bath, 65 francs; double with bath, 120 francs. It's down the hill behind the station.

To reach the base of the Landwasser Viaduct, follow the footpath or the road down into the village of Filisur. Walk west along the highway that comes into town. Cross the river, then turn right on a dirt road that follows the river into the woods. In about five minutes you'll reach a signpost pointing to Schmitten. Follow the path a minute or two, and you'll get a good view of the west side of the viaduct. The views are somewhat obstructed by trees, but the bridge is impressive nonetheless. The path will take you up to track level and beyond, but hiking boots are recommended. Time from the station to the view point is 30-40 minutes. The walk back up to the Filisur station takes longer.

ST. MORITZ

Chur	leave	0855	0955	1052	(S940, C540)
St. Moritz	arrive	1053	1153	1253	
St. Moritz	leave	1200	hourly	2000	
Chur	arrive	1405	until	2206	

Several trains between Chur and St. Moritz carry restaurant cars, but their operation appears to depend on the season and the number of restaurant cars working on the Glacier Express. If you can't get a restaurant car reservation on the Glacier Express, a meal on a St. Moritz train is a most acceptable substitute.

Chur to Filisur

Distance: 51 km
Company: RhB (meter gauge)
Maximum grade: 35 per mill

It was proposed to extend the Landquart–Davos line to St. Moritz or into Italy, and another route was proposed from Chur through Filisur to Samedan in the Inn valley. Construction of the latter line began in 1894, following the Rhein from Landquart through Chur (14 kilometers) to Reichenau, then following the Hinter Rhein to Thusis, 41 kilometers from Landquart. The line was opened in the summer of 1896. In November of that year the Landquart-Davos Railway changed its name to Rhätische Bahn (Rhaetian Railway in English, Ferrovia Retica in Italian, Viafier Retica in Rhaeto-Romansh).

Construction of the extension from Thusis along the Albula River through Filisur to Samedan began in 1898. There are numerous stone bridges, best-known of which is the Landwasser Viaduct at Filisur. The line was opened in 1903.

The Landwasser Viaduct is the one you've seen on the travel posters. It is built on a radius of 100 meters, and the south end (toward Filisur) springs right from the wall of the gorge. For the best view from a St. Moritz-bound train, sit on the right. The viaduct comes only a minute or two before Filisur; the station before the viaduct is Alvaneu. The train pictured is heading for Filisur and St. Moritz on September 9, 1991.

The line is dual gauge from Chur to Domat/Ems, 6.5 kilometers, so SBB can have access to industries there. The grade is no more than 25 per mill as far as Filisur, junction with the line that comes down the Landwasser valley from Davos (opened 1909).

Filisur to Samedan, Pontresina, and St. Moritz

Just above Filisur is a spiral tunnel. The grade steepens to 35 per mill. More tunnels follow. Beyond Bergün the line doubles back on itself and a few kilometers farther passes through three spiral tunnels, crossing and recrossing the valley. The 5.8-kilometer Albula Tunnel is the longest straight stretch on the RhB.

From the tunnel down to Samedan, only 6 kilometers, the line is almost anticlimactic.

Samedan

The main line from Chur joins the Engadine line from Scuol-Tarasp to St. Moritz at Bever, 2 kilometers northeast of Samedan — the curve at Bever is the sharpest on the main line. A branch diverges to Pontresina at the west end of the Samedan station. It carries shuttle trains to Pontresina and the Bernina Express trains. Samedan has an engine terminal, shop, and dispatching center.

Opposite the station in Samedan is the Hotel Terminus. I haven't stayed there, but I ate well there in 1988.

• Hotel Terminus (**), Via Retica 24, CH-7503 Samedan. Phone 41-82-6 53 36, fax 6 44 52. Single with bath, 97-102 francs; double with bath, 188-196 francs; rates include dinner.

St. Moritz

It's 5 kilometers from Samedan through Celerina to St. Moritz. To the south you can see the Bernina line coming into St. Moritz from Pontresina.

St. Moritz is one of the winter playgrounds of Europe — at least of wealthy Europe. I always seem to visit the town off season, possibly because that's when it's affordable. The main part of town is on the hillside above the station.

There are two hotels at station level. Friends recommend the Hotel Bellaval, between the station and the lake, as comfortable and relatively inexpensive. On the side of the station toward the town is the Hotel La Margna. Other friends have mentioned the Waldhaus am See, a little beyond the Bellaval and across a bridge.

• Hotel Bellaval (**), Via Grevas 55, CH-7500 St. Moritz. Phone 41-81-833 32 45, fax 833 04 06. Single without bath, 62-75 francs; double with bath, 154-180 francs; without bath, 120-140 francs.

• Hotel La Margna (****), Via Serlas 5, CH-7500 St. Moritz. Phone 41-81-832 21 41, fax 833 16 72. Single with bath, 170-210 francs; double with bath, 320-400 francs; rates include dinner.

• Hotel Waldhaus am See (***), Via Dim Lei 6, CH-7500 St. Moritz. Phone 41-81-833 76 76, fax 833 88 77. Single with bath, 150-180 francs; double with bath, 260-330 francs; rates include dinner.

If you are staying in St. Moritz or Samedan, RhB's Engadine line to Scuol-Tarasp makes a nice morning or afternoon ride.

St. Moritz	leave	0842	1342	RhB (S960, C546)
Samedan	leave	0855	1355	
Scuol-Tarasp	arrive	1010	1510	

Scuol-Tarasp	leave	1050	1550
Samedan	arrive	1205	1705
St. Moritz	arrive	1218	1718

TIRANO

Bernina Express

Chur	leave	0848	0855	(S940, C540
Tirano	arrive	1240	1328	(S950, C547)
Tirano	leave	1405	1445	
Chur	arrive	1905	1853	

Heidiland/Bernina Express

Chur	leave	0716	SBB (S900, C520)
Landquart	arrive	0724	
Landquart	leave	0745	RhB (S910, C545)
Tirano	arrive	1224	(S950, C547)
Tirano	leave	1405	
Landquart	arrive	1901	
Landquart	leave	1934	
Chur	arrive	1944	

The Bernina Expresses from Chur at 0848 and from Tirano at 1445 run only in the summer and have a 6-franc supplemental fare which includes a seat reservation. In winter the 1405 from Tirano is replaced by a train at 1430 (same arrival time in Chur). The Heidiland/Bernina Express operates between Landquart and Tirano via Davos and Filisur during the summer. The through-car arrangements for the Bernina Expresses are complicated and depend on the season. Read the footnotes carefully. Or take one of the local trains — the scenery will be just the same. Some trains on the Bernina line carry open observation cars in good weather during the summer.

Samedan and St. Moritz to Pontresina and Tirano

Distances:

Samedan–Pontresina: 5 km

St. Moritz–Pontresina: 6 km

Pontresina–Tirano: 55 km

Company: RhB

Maximum grade: 70 per mill

The southeast portion of Graubunden is geographically part of Italy. A railway was necessary to supplement the postal road because of the height of Bernina Pass, the severe weather, and the great distances between towns. The Bernina Railway was organized in 1904. It was planned to start from Samedan, but the terminal was moved to St. Moritz as a consequence of the construction of RhB's branch from Samedan to Pontresina.

The builders considered rack operation over about one-fifth of the line. However, the eventual cost of carrying the weight of the extra equipment over the rest of the line led them to lengthen the line somewhat and reduce the grade (if a 7 percent grade can be considered reduced). The builders also considered a summit tunnel. They realized it would eliminate some scenery and thus cut tourist traffic. Also (possibly chiefly) it would be expensive to build. The resulting line overcomes by adhesion a greater difference in height than any rack railway in Switzerland (from Tirano at 429 meters to Ospizio Bernina at 2,253 meters — a difference of 1,824 meters or 5,983 feet).

The line was completed in 1910. RhB took over operation of the line at the beginning of 1942, and it absorbed the corporation on January 1, 1943. The Bernina line is electrified at 1000 volts DC, so its motor cars don't stray onto the rest of the RhB.

The 70 per mill grade starts at the south end of the Pontresina station. The grade eases to 43 per mill for 5 kilometers (you'll see the Morteratsch Glacier to the south). The 70 per mill resumes as the line climbs well above treeline.

The summit is at Bernina Hospiz (Ospizio Bernina), 2,253 meters above sea level (7,390 feet). The descent at 70 per mill begins and continues almost constantly to Poschiavo. The views are spectacular. There are horseshoe tunnels at Alp Grüm and Cadera. There is a hiking trail from Ospizio to Alp Grüm. The walk takes about 90 minutes. Hiking boots are recommended.

Almost 8 kilometers of easier grade follows Poschiavo along the shore of the Lake of Poschiavo, then the 70 per mill resumes, with a complete loop at Brusio, described by someone in one of my tour groups as "an open-air spiral tunnel." It's Tehachapi Loop on a smaller scale.

A 12-minute walk from the Brusio station down through the village will bring you to the loop. Allow at least 15 minutes for the walk back up to the station. There is a cafe next to the station and another down in the village.

Tirano

The last 2 kilometers of the line are in Italy. Border-crossing formalities are done in the RhB station. You'll have time for a pizza and a beer in one of the restaurants along the street that runs north from the station plaza, then maybe a gelato (ice cream) and a look around the FS (Italian State Railways) station before you board the train back to Chur or St. Moritz. The restaurants and gelaterias gladly accept Swiss francs. I wouldn't want to recommend one of those restaurants over another without sampling their pizza and beer several more times.

GENÈVE

Genève — that's the French spelling. You know it as Geneva, but when you get there the signs will say "Genève." If you board the train in the German-speaking area, you may have to look for a train going to Genf; south of the Alps it's Ginevra. I haven't stayed there; indeed, I've spent barely an hour there. I've included it for a few rail-oriented items there and nearby.

The main station in Genève is also used by French National Railways — lots of TGVs and ordinary equipment too. The SBB line west of Genève is electrified at 1,500 volts DC, the French voltage, and SBB has a small fleet of 1,500-volt cars that run in local service as far as La Plaine.

Most SBB long-distance trains do not terminate or originate at Cornavin Station, the main station, but at Cointrin Airport, 6 minutes away.

Between Genève and Lausanne two meter-gauge lines head toward the mountains, the Nyon–St-Cergue–Morez from Nyon and the Bière-Apples-Morges from Morges. I've ridden the BAM a couple of stations out and the NStCM all the way. It's possible to do both these in a day from Aigle or Bern, too.

There is boat service on Lac Léman (table S3150) connecting Genève, Nyon, Morges, and Lausanne. It makes a nice change of pace to walk down to the lake and ride a boat.

HOTELS

• Hotel Bernina (✳✳), 22 place Cornavin, CH-1201 Genève; phone 41-22-731 49 50, fax 732 73 59. Single with bath, 105-125 francs; without bath, 80-85 francs; double with bath, 140-168 francs; without bath, 105-125 francs. It is opposite the southeast corner of the station.

Off the southwest corner of the station are:

• Hotel Astoria (✳✳✳), 6 place Cornavin, CH-1211 Genève 1; phone 41-22-732 10 25, fax 731 76 90. Single with bath, 115-160 francs; double with bath, 155-200 francs.

• Hotel Suisse (✳✳✳), 10 place Cornavin, CH-1201 Genève; phone 41-22-732 66 30, fax 732 62 39. Single with bath, 135-160 francs; double with bath, 180-200 francs.

• West of the station is the Hotel Cornavin (✳✳✳✳), Place de la Gare Cornavin, CH-1201 Genève; phone 41-22-732 21 00, fax 732 88 43. Single with bath, 140-195 francs; double with bath, 185-260 francs.

RAILWAY COMPANIES IN ADDITION TO SBB
French National Railways (SNCF)

RECOMMENDED TRIPS
Morges–Bière
Nyon–La Cure
Rhône Valley

MORGES–BIÈRE

Genève	leave	0918	SBB (S150, C505)
Morges	arrive	0946	
Morges	leave	0953	BAM (S156, C502)
Bière	arrive	1021	
Bière	leave	1048	
Morges	arrive	1118	
Morges	leave	1144	
Genève	arrive	1214	

Distance: 19 km
Company: Bière-Apples-Morges
Maximum grade: 35 per mill

The BAM is a bifurcated line, dividing at Apples to Bière (the main route) and L'Isle (branch line), and it doesn't do nearly as much climbing as the NStCM. Even so, it has a fairly steady climb at about 35 per mill up over two summits beyond Apples. The 11-km branch from Apples to L'Isle is more or less level.

The BAM was built in 1895 and 1896. It was electrified in 1943 using SBB's 15,000-volt system. BAM's bright green cars have an interesting coupling device on the ends for hauling standard-gauge cars on transporters (as near as I can tell), and at Morges you can see dual-gauge track. The BAM handles a lot of military traffic to the depot at Bière. At Vufflens-le-Chateau, the first station out of Morges, you can get photos of the train with a large castle in the background. For a hotel recommendation for Morges, see page 108.

NYON–LA CURE

Genève	leave	0918	SBB (S150, C505)
Nyon	arrive	0931	
Nyon	leave	0935	NStCM (S155, C501)
La Cure	arrive	1022	
La Cure	leave	1035	
Nyon	arrive	1123	
Nyon	leave	1127	
Genève	arrive	1142	

Distance: 27 km
Company: NStCM
Maximum grade: 60 per mill

Board the red-and-orange cars of the NStCM at the curb across the street from the SBB station. The line winds back and forth as it climbs from 406 meters at Nyon to a summit of 1,233 meters beyond La Givrine, then descends to 1,155 meters at La Cure. There are views of Lac Léman and Mont Blanc on the way in good weather. The line ends right at the French border. There's not much at La Cure; St. Cergue is a larger town. It is hard to find anything open for a late lunch in Nyon.

Construction of the NStCM began in 1912. The line was opened to St. Cergue, now a ski resort, in 1916, and to the French border in 1917. The French portion of the line to Morez was opened in 1921, and that section of the line was closed in 1958. However, the railway still retains the destination in its name. The NStCM was electrified from the beginning, and it has been modernized in recent years.

RHÔNE VALLEY

The excursions described from Montreux, Aigle, Bex, and Martigny can be made from Genève. Departure times for Genève are shown in that section. See pages 122-129.

STREETCARS

Said a fervent young Calvinist, "Damn!
I've just realized that I am
*   A person who moves*
*   In predestinate grooves —*
I'm not even a bus, I'm a tram!"

Appropriately for the home of John Calvin, there are trams on the streets — Lines 12, 13, and 16 of the Genève transportation system. Table S992.70 of the bus volume lists the routes.

As near as I can tell from that listing and the map in a 7-year-old Michelin green guide, all three routes connect at Plainpalais, south of the Rhône. Line 13 runs from Palettes through Bachet, Carouge, and Plainpalais to Cornavin, the main railway station. Line 12 originates at Bachet, follows the same route to Plainpalais, then goes out to, through, or past Bel Air and Rive to Moillesulaz. Line 16 runs from Augustins to Plainpalais, then joins route 12 to Moillesulaz.

THE GLACIER EXPRESS

The Glacier Express is like a Swiss California Zephyr (the pre-Amtrak CZ). It is operated by the Rhaetian, Furka-Oberalp, and Brig-Visp-Zermatt railways, which correspond to the Burlington, Rio Grande, and Western Pacific if you let your imagination run loose.

The Rhein and Rhône valleys form a long trench through the Alps from Chur southwest to Brig. The two watersheds are separated by the Furka and Oberalp passes, between which lies the town of Andermatt in the Reuss valley. The Chur–Brig route is an important one, and many of Switzerland's military installations are situated along it. Their presence may be in large measure the reason for the construction of the Furka Base Tunnel, which permits year-round operation of the line between Oberwald and Andermatt.

Between Chur and Brig the Glacier Express runs as a separate train. Between Brig and Zermatt the through coaches are attached to regular trains. Cars to and from St. Moritz are switched in and out of regular RhB expresses at Chur or Reichenau-Tamins — and if the train is late, switching scheduled for Chur may be done at Reichenau instead.

Some of the Glacier Expresses offer Panorama cars. With their huge windows and supplemental windows in the roof they offer superb viewing, but the seating is 2-and-2, even in first class, and the windows don't open.

Most Glacier Express trains carry a restaurant car for part of the trip. The cars range from nicely restored older cars to a new two-unit car. Meals are sometimes also served in the Panorama car that's next to the restaurant car. I regret to report that one of the dining cars has been painted mauve outside.

Reservations are necessary for the restaurant car because tour groups book space long in advance and the capacity of the cars, even the new two-unit car, is much less than the capacity of the train. For reservations, call SSG, the Swiss Dining Car Company, in Chur at 81-252 14 25.

In October 1997 the table d'hote lunch cost 34 francs; beverages are extra (a bottle of mineral water and a cup of coffee were another 7.20). The souvenir slanted wineglass is 15 francs.

Reservations are required for coach seats, too. The charge is 9 francs. Consider the non-reserved local trains instead. You'll have more room and you'll get a longer look at the scenery.

The Glacier Expresses do not carry checked baggage — it moves on local trains or goes the long way around.

Eastbound schedules

Glacier Express		A	B	C	D	
Zermatt	leave	0815	0849	0949	1015	(S140, S611, C576)
Brig	arrive	0942	1015	1115	1142	
Brig	leave	0955	1030	1130	1151	(S610, S611, C575)
Disentis	arrive	1237	1300	1433	1437	
Disentis	leave	1315	1315	1443	1500	(S920, S611C540)
Chur	arrive	1431	1431	1556	I	
Chur	leave		1452		I	
St. Moritz	arrive		1653		1811	

Glacier Express D operates year round and arrives Chur at 1610 during the winter (St. Moritz cars are switched out at Reichenau-Tamins). The other trains operate from the beginning of June to mid-October.

Westbound schedules

Glacier Express		F	G	H	K
St. Moritz	leave			0930	1000
Chur	arrive			I	1205
Chur	leave	0857	1057	I	1220
Disentis	arrive	1010	1208	1222	1335
Disentis	leave	1022	1220	1242	1345
Brig	arrive	1311	1510	1531	1614
Brig	leave	1318	1518	1549	1633
Zermatt	arrive	1442	1642	1713	1753

Glacier Express G runs year round, and during the winter the 0900 train from St. Moritz carries a first-class Panoroma car that is switched into the Glacier Express at Reichenau-Tamins. The other trains operate from the beginning of June to mid-October.

Chur to Disentis

Distance: 59 km
Company: Rhaetian Railway (RhB)
Maximum grade: 27 per mill

The line along the Vorder Rhein from Reichenau-Tamins to Ilanz opened in 1903 and from Ilanz to Disentis (Mustér in Romansh) in 1912. It diverges from the line to St. Moritz at Reichenau-Tamins, at the confluence of the Vorder Rhein and the Hinter Rhein (Front Rhine and Back Rhine). A little west of there the line passes the Flims Landslip, where in prehistoric times part of a mountain fell into the river. The line climbs steadily along the Vorder Rhein. The grade is 10 per mill to Ilanz, which is considered the first town on the Rhine. The grade increases a little there, and from Trun to Disentis it is 27 per mill.

An eastbound Glacier Express departs from Reichenau-Tamins on the last leg of its run to Chur in March 1993. The Rhätische Bahn is heavy-duty mainline railroading on rails 1 meter apart

Disentis to Brig

Distance: 97 km
Company: Furka-Oberalp (FO)
Maximum grade: 110 per mill (R)

The Swiss Furka Railway Company was formed in 1910 to build from Brig along the Rhône and over or under Furka and Oberalp passes to Disentis. It was opened from Brig to Gletsch in 1914. The company went bankrupt in 1923 with the Furka Tunnel (the old one at the top of the pass) still incomplete.

Meanwhile, the Schöllenen Railway (SchB) was built and opened in 1917 from Göschenen, at the north portal of the Gotthard Tunnel, up to Andermatt, 3.75 kilometers with a maximum grade of 179 per mill.

In 1925 a syndicate that included the RhB, SchB, and Visp-Zermatt Railway formed the Furka-Oberalp Railway to take over the Swiss Furka Railway. Construction resumed, and the FO opened from Brig through Andermatt to Disentis on July 4, 1926. Through service between St. Moritz and Zermatt began in 1930 after the VZ completed an extension from Visp to Brig.

The FO was electrified between 1940 and 1942. At the end of 1960 the FO acquired the SchB and became independent from the Brig-Visp-Zermatt. The 15.41-kilometer Furka Base Tunnel between Oberwald and Realp opened in June 1982, and the line over Furka Pass (which passed several glaciers, from which the train got its name) was abandoned. The old line had to be closed each winter, and had a bridge that had to be dismantled each fall to let avalanches pass. Part of that line is being restored as a museum, with steam locomotives brought back from Viet Nam, where they went when FO electrified (see page 71).

As the train leaves Disentis it enters a tunnel and begins a section of rack operation. The station names look like no language you've ever seen — it's Rhaeto-Romansh, Switzerland's one-percent minority language. Soon the train reaches the summit of Oberalp Pass (2,033 meters), where the line runs along the edge of a small lake, then enters an avalanche gallery. Then the descent to Andermatt begins, eventually at 110 per mill, just like the ascent. Both sides of the train afford a good view as the line loops back and forth.

At Andermatt the train connects with trains to and from Göschenen on the Gotthard main line, 3.75 kilometers north and 330 meters down. From Andermatt the train has a short, relatively easy run to the Furka Base Tunnel. Inside the tunnel are two passing sidings, and it's likely your train will meet another in there. In the 41 kilometers from the west portal to Brig there are two sections of rack operation totaling about 5 kilometers of grade up to 90 per mill, and there is a spiral tunnel between Lax and Grengiols. Just before reaching Brig you can look to the left and see the north portals of the Simplon Tunnel.

The train changes ends at Brig because of the track layout. The FO-BVZ tracks at Brig are in the plaza in front of the station. There is a proposal to remove the tracks from the street and put them up with the standard-gauge lines.

For a description of the line from Brig to Zermatt, turn to the section on Zermatt, page 142. The Chur–St. Moritz route is covered on pages 81-83.

THE GOTTHARD ROUTE

The Gotthard Route is the principal north-south route through Switzerland. It is outstandingly scenic, and much of it is accessible by train for lineside photography. For the most part, these hotel listings and notes on good photo locations are taken from a special issue of the German magazine *Eisenbahn Kurier*. (The special edition, No. 1175, dated December 1990/January/February 1991, is still available. Write to *Eisenbahn Kurier* at Postfach 5560, 79022 Freiburg, Germany. The price is 24.80 deutsche marks.)

HISTORY

A north-south line through the Alps had been proposed as early as 1848, and a route along the Reuss and Ticino valleys was chosen in 1869. The Italian, German, and Swiss governments all helped finance its construction.

The original route lay from Luzern through Rotkreuz and along the west shore of the Zuger See; the more direct route through Meggen and Küssnacht was opened in 1897. The shapes of the lakes and the mountains are such that it takes about 25 miles of train riding to get from Luzern to Brunnen, about 15 miles straight-line distance.

Work on the Gotthard Tunnel from Göschenen to Airolo was begun in June 1872, and the line was opened for full service just 10 years later. The Gotthard Tunnel is double track. At the apex, about the midpoint, is a pair of crossovers. The ascending grade southward in the tunnel is 6 per mill; the northward ascending grade is only 2 per mill.

THE LINE

Routes from Luzern and Zurich meet at Arth-Goldau, north of Mount Rigi. The line detours to the east around Rigi and Hochfluh (the mountain west of Schwyz), passes through the town of Schwyz, then returns to the shore of the Vierwaldstätter See (Lake Luzern) at Brunnen. It follows the lake south through Sisikon to Flüelen. The southward track is the newer of the two and in tunnel much of the way; the northward track offers better views of the lake. From Flüelen the line continues south-south-east along the River Reuss, climbing at 10 per mill.

The grade begins in earnest at Erstfeld — 26 per mill all the way to Göschenen, with a few short stretches of 27 and 28 per mill. South of Gurtnellen the line has a spiral tunnel. Just south of that is the village of Wassen, which the line passes three times.

Southbound travelers see the church up on the hillside to their right, then at the same level as the train, again on the right, then down below on the left. The line continues climbing, mostly in a tunnel, to Göschenen. The grade ends just north of the station.

At Göschenen a short, steep branch of the meter gauge Furka-Oberalp Railway meets the Gotthard Route. In 3.75 kilometers it climbs 330 meters up the Schöllenen Gorge to a junction with FO's main route at Andermatt. The maximum grade is 179 per mill (17.9 percent). The parallel highway has to go through all kinds of contortions.

Partway up is the Devil's Bridge. The legend is that the devil allowed the bridge to be built in exchange for the first being to cross it. The canny Swiss by then had read what happened to Jephthah (Judges 11:30-39) and let a goat precede the humans.

The south portal of the tunnel is at Airolo. There the line turns almost due east and begins its descent along the Ticino River. The grade ranges from 25 to 28 per mill. North of Faido is a pair of spiral tunnels; between Lavorgo and Giornico are two more — and stacked, to boot. It is possible to see and photograph three levels of track at once. The grade abates north of Biasca; from there to Bellinzona it ranges from 6 to 10 per mill.

The line climbs from 436 meters at Flüelen to 1,106 meters at Göschenen, 670 meters in 38 kilometers. Northbound trains climb from 230 meters at Giubiasco, south of Bellinzona, to 1,141 meters at Airolo (SBB's highest station), 911 meters in 68 kilometers. (The apex of the tunnel is at 1,151 meters.) The 145-kilometer stretch from Arth-Goldau to Giubiasco is the longest without a junction in Switzerland.

The Gotthard line is far busier and much steeper than any similar line in the U.S. The line is pretty much a one-speed railroad, and freight-train length is restricted to permit passenger-train speeds.

FOOD AND LODGING

Three cities in this guide can serve as base camps for exploring the Gotthard Route: Luzern, Zürich, and Lugano. Erstfeld, where the southbound climb starts, is about an hour from Luzern and somewhat more than that from Zurich. Northbound, the climb starts at Biasca, about 40 minutes north of Lugano.

Consider staying in one of the towns along the route instead. The listings below are arranged from north to south. The listing of the hotels is a short one. There are more hotels out there, and during most of the year an advance reservation is not necessary. You're never far from food and lodging.

A freight train carrying new automobiles rolls north past the Hotel Bahnhof in Sisikon on October 13, 1987.

InterCity trains on the route stop at Arth-Goldau, Bellinzona, Lugano, and Chiasso. Semi-fast trains stop at all the towns listed but Sisikon. Local trains run between Arth-Goldau and Erstfeld (some go only as far as Flüelen), between Bellinzona and Lugano, and between Lugano and Chiasso. For places between Erstfeld and Göschenen use the hourly bus service shown in bus timetable S600.32. A similar local bus service runs hourly on the south ramp of the pass between Airolo and Bellinzona (bus timetable S625.09).

Sisikon

Sisikon is a special case — perhaps the ultimate railroad-enthusiast hotel. In several books and magazines I saw pictures of trains passing through Sisikon. Right next to the tracks was a building with a sign on the roof: "Hotel." I found the town on the map: south of Arth-Goldau and north of Erstfeld. I looked up Sisikon in the *Swiss Hotel Guide* and found a single hotel, the Tellsplatte. I wrote for a reservation and enclosed a copy of the page in *Eisenbahn Kurier*. I got a letter from Antoinette Gick, manager of the Hotel Bahnhof, saying that the manager of the Tellsplatte had sent the letter to her and that she had reserved me a room with a balcony that had a view of the lake, the mountains, and the railway. Indeed, the view included the signal for southbound trains; when it was green I knew there'd be a train along within minutes. One evening I counted 14 trains between 9 and 10 o'clock. I slept better the second night.

On the minus side there's not much in Sisikon: post office, grocery store, a few other hotels and restaurants. The main north-south road runs through the village, and the traffic is noisy.

• Hotel Bahnhof, CH-6452 Sisikon, phone 41-41-820 12 84, fax 820 52 21. Single with bath, 65 francs; double with bath, 85 francs. The hotel restaurant has closed (the proprietors are easing into retirement), but there are other restaurants nearby. Apartments are available for extended stays.

Flüelen

Four hotels are opposite the station, and you can probably ask for rooms with a view of the tracks.

• Hostellerie Sternen (✻✻✻), Axenstrasse 6, CH-6456 Flüelen, phone 41-41-875 03 03, fax 875 03 05. Single with bath, 115-140 francs; double with bath, 165-210 francs.

• Weisses Kreuz (✻✻), Axenstrasse 2, CH-6454 Flüelen, phone 41-41-870 17 17, fax 870 17 75. Single with bath, 75-85 francs; double with bath, 120-130 francs.

• Tell & Post, Axenstrasse 12, CH-6454 Flüelen, phone 41-41-874 11 30. Single with bath, 70-80 francs; without bath, 60-70 francs; double with bath, 115-130 francs; without bath, 102-112 francs.

• Hotel Hirschen — not listed in the *Swiss Hotel Guide*.

Erstfeld

Three hotels are right behind the station:

• Hotel Frohsinn (✻✻), CH-6472 Erstfeld, phone 41-41-882 01 01, fax 882 01 00, fax 5 11 94. Single with bath, 53-57 francs; double with bath, 98-106 francs.

• Hotel Bahnhof — not listed in the *Swiss Hotel Guide*.

• Hotel Hirschen — also not listed, but a railfan favorite, according to *Eisenbahn Kurier,* and only a Katzensprung from the station. ("Katzensprung" is a German word meaning from the floor to the middle of the dining table or from the stove to the top of the refrigerator.)

Göschenen
• Zum Weissen Rössli (∗∗∗), CH-6487 Göschenen, phone 41-41-886 80 10, fax 886 80 30. Single with bath, 90-110 francs; double with bath, 180-210 francs.
• Gotthard (∗), CH-6487 Göschenen, phone 41-41-885 12 63, fax 885 17 65. Single with bath, 51-54 francs, without bath, 42-45 francs; double with bath, 89-95 francs, without bath, 79-85 francs.
• Hotel Löwen and Hotel Krone — neither is listed in the *Swiss Hotel Guide.*

You'll find railroad art on the walls of the station buffet; there are tables on the platform.

Airolo
• Forni (∗∗∗), Via Stazione, CH-6780 Airolo, phone 41-91-869 12 70, fax 869 15 23. Single with bath, 75-100 francs; double with bath, 130-160 francs. I am guessing from the location on Via Stazione (Station Street) that it's not far from the station.

Faido
• The Hotel Milano, CH-6760 Faido, is right behind the station, but it is not listed in the *Swiss Hotel Guide.*

Biasca
• Albergo Nazionale (∗∗), Bellinzona 24, CH-6710 Biasca, phone 41-91-862 13 31, fax 862 43 62. Single with bath, 90-110 francs; without bath, 50-60 francs; double with bath, 130-170 francs; without bath, 90-110 francs. It is directly behind the station.
• Nearby is the Albergo della Posta — it is not listed in the *Swiss Hotel Guide.*

PHOTO SPOTS
Photographing trains on the Gotthard route is the opposite of chasing the sole train of the day on an American branch line. Chasing is futile because of the speeds and unnecessary because of the frequency of trains. Choose one or two locations for the day and spend several hours.

The north ramp of the pass has had far more attention from railfans than the south ramp, but the south ramp is more likely to have better weather and better lighting. In addition the south ramp has more spiral tunnels and crosses the valley more often.

Among the more-frequented spots, judging by the number of pictures I've seen are:

• Sisikon: The highway south of the village passes over the tunnel portals, affording good views of southbound trains. The light is better in the afternoon.

• Wassen: The churchyard affords a view of the middle and upper levels as they cross the Meienreuss (it's a morning location). With luck you can catch trains on both bridges at once. Roads wind around the village, affording access to different vantage points. The interior of the church is worth a look. Local trains no longer serve Wassen. You'll need to take the substitute bus.

• Göschenen: I've seen a number of photos taken from directly above the tunnel portals looking north into the station.

• Lavorgo and Giornico: The double spiral tunnels are about halfway between these two stations, which are about 5 kilometers apart, straight-line distance, measuring on the map. Lavorgo is the more likely of the two places to have a taxi that could take you to a good spot.

• Bellinzona: Directly south of the station is a tunnel, above which is a castle; south of that tunnel is a good photo spot.

Among the other stations that afford good photos either from the platforms or nearby are Arth-Goldau, Steinen, Schwyz, Intschi, Gurtnellen, Airolo, and Faido.

VICARIOUS RAILFANNING

The Transport Museum at Luzern offers you a ride with the engineer up the north ramp of the Gotthard line in a movie theater that includes a replica of a locomotive cab. A large HO-scale model railroad depicts the same portion of the line.

INTERLAKEN

Interlaken lies between the Lake of Thun and the Lake of Brienz (Thuner See and Brienzer See). Both lakes have boat service. The town has been a resort for a long time, and there are areas that look like every other resort. There are two stations, West and Ost (East). West is at the center of town; Ost is on the north edge and is the junction of the standard gauge Bern-Lötschberg-Simplon, the meter gauge Berner Oberland-Bahnen, and the meter gauge SBB line over Brünig Pass to Luzern.

A model railroad open to the public, the Modelleisenbahn-Treff Interlaken, is about 3 minutes' walk west (that's railroad west but compass south) of the Interlaken West station, more or less opposite the Migros store. It is open 1000-1200 and 1330-1800 from the end of April to mid-October. Admission is 6 francs.

At Brienz on the Brünig line is the Ballenberg Open-Air Museum of Rural culture. Buses run from Brienz to the museum (table 470.92). The museum is open from mid-April through October.

HOTELS

• Bernerhof (∗∗∗), Bahnhofstrasse 16, CH-3800 Interlaken, phone 41-36-22 31 31, fax 22 84 28. Single with bath, 110-150 francs; double with bath, 185-240 francs. The Bernerhof was memorable in 1986 for an excellent breakfast buffet (don't get up so late you miss the bread pudding) and was even better in 1993, 1994, and 1995. The rooms are smallish, but the people who run the hotel are as nice as they come. When the tour group left, they came out on the balcony and waved good bye. The restaurant on the ground floor is quite good.

• Toscana (∗∗∗), Jungfraustrasse 19, CH-3800 Interlaken, phone 41-36-23 30 33, fax 23 35 51. Single with bath, 108-146 francs; double with bath, 166-220 francs. I haven't stayed at the Toscana, but I have eaten well in its restaurant almost every time I have been in Interlaken. I should think the food would speak for the accommodations.

• Hotel Interlaken (∗∗∗∗), Höheweg 74, CH-3800 Interlaken, phone 41-36-21 22 11, fax 23 31 21. Single with bath, 130-178 francs; double with bath, 218-294 francs. The Hotel Interlaken, the oldest hotel in Interlaken, is near the east end of the Höheweg, about 5 minutes' walk from the Interlaken Ost station.

• Hotel Weisses Kreuz (∗∗∗), Am Höheweg, CH-3800 Interlaken, phone 41-36-22 59 51, fax 23 35 55. Single with bath, 108-146 francs; double with bath, 166-220 francs. I have not stayed at the Weisses Kreuz, but I ate well there.

Across from the Interlaken West station are two hotels I have not tried, but their location commends them.

• Hotel Merkur (∗∗∗), Bahnhofstrasse 35, CH-3800 Interlaken, phone 41-36-22 66 55, fax 22 66 16. Single with bath 116-159 francs; double with bath, 190-250 francs.

• Hotel Eden-Nova, (∗∗∗), Bahnhofplatz 45, CH-3800 Interlaken, phone 41-36-22 88 12, fax 22 88 68. Single with bath, 108-144 francs; double with bath, 156-225 francs.

HOTELS NEAR INTERLAKEN

A friend spoke well of the Jungfrau Hotel in Wilderswil, 5 minutes from Interlaken Ost on

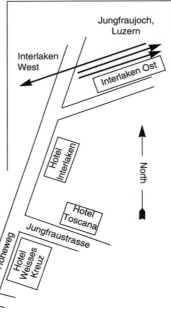

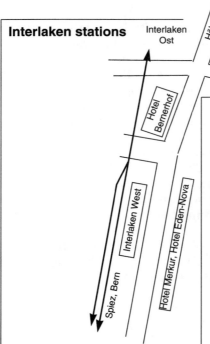

the BOB at the junction of the line to Schynige Platte. In addition to trains, BOB operates two or three buses every hour between Interlaken West and Wilderswil (S300.80).

• Hotel Jungfrau (∗∗∗∗), CH-3812 Wilderswil), phone 41-36-22 35 31, fax 22 72 92. Single with bath, 100-120 francs; double with bath, 170-200 francs.

If you want to stay up in the mountains, beyond

the reach of automobiles but not beyond the reach of the Swiss Pass, consider Wengen, above Lauterbrunnen.

• Hotel Regina (∗∗∗∗), CH-3823 Wengen; phone 41-36-55 15 12, fax 55 15 74. Single with bath, 133-151 francs; double with bath, 235-338 francs (prices are non-skiing season). The Regina is uphill from the WAB station (tables S311 and C564) and offers magnificent views across the valley to Mürren. When I stayed there in 1991, the permanent residents included a large friendly dog and two kittens.

• Hotel Falken (∗∗∗), CH-3823 Wengen; phone 41-36-56 51 21, fax 55 33 39. Single with bath, 140-160 francs, without bath, 120-140 francs; double with bath, 270-330 francs, without bath 240-280 francs (prices are for midsummer).

RAILWAY COMPANIES IN ADDITION TO SBB

Bern-Lötschberg-Simplon (BLS) — standard gauge
Berner Oberland-Bahnen (BOB) — meter gauge
SBB's line to Interlaken is meter gauge

RECOMMENDED TRIPS

Brienzer Rothorn
Jungfraujoch
Luzern
Mürren and Schilthorn

BRIENZER ROTHORN

Interlaken West	leave	1212	BLS (S310, C560)
Interlaken Ost	arrive	1215	
Interlaken Ost	leave	1219	SBB (S470, C561)
Brienz	arrive	1237	
Brienz	leave	1255	BRB (S475)
Rothorn Kulm	arrive	1355	
Rothorn Kulm	leave	1430	
Brienz	arrive	1530	
Brienz	leave	1622	
Interlaken Ost	arrive	1640	
Interlaken Ost	leave	1645	
Interlaken West	arrive	1648	

Brienz to Rothorn Kulm

Distance: 8 km
Company: Brienz-Rothorn Bahn (BRB)
Track gauge: 800 mm (31.5 inches)
Maximum grade: 250 per mill (rack)
Season: early June to mid-October

Steam locomotives work several trips each day on the BRB; diesels cover the rest. The line's newest steam locomotive was built by SLM of Winterthur in 1991. Round trip fare from Brienz to Rothorn Kulm (summit, culmination) was 54 francs a few years ago. The Swiss Pass map doesn't show the line, so there may be no discount even with the pass. Schedules depend on the weather and on the amount of business — there are trains before and after those shown (I cited a mid-day schedule because mornings tend to be cloudy). Check the Interlaken–Brienz schedules too — the summer season brings changes, especially on the weekends.

The ride offers magnificent views once it climbs out of the forest above Brienz, and there's a restaurant up top.

The Swiss Pass is valid on the boats between Brienz and Interlaken Ost (table S3470). There's a boat from Brienz, right in front of the station, at 1605; it arrives Interlaken Ost at 1725 after backing a considerable distance down the river between the Brienzer See and the Thuner See. The 1605 trip is operated with a steamer during much of the season.

JUNGFRAUJOCH

Important! The Swiss Pass is valid only as far as Wengen and Grindelwald; the Eurailpass, *not at all*. You must buy tickets for the remainder of the trip. The round-trip fare from Interlaken Ost to Jungfraujoch is 163.60 francs first class (and first class cars are available only to Lauterbrunnen and Grindelwald), 153.20 francs second class. The Swiss Pass and the various Eurail passes yield a discount — show them when you buy the ticket. The Wengen–Jungfraujoch–Grindelwald fare is probably less. Get up early, check the weather (you don't want to spend all that money riding through clouds), and go to the station early enough to get the tickets. If the weather is iffy, ride to Wengen on your Swiss Pass, buy a ticket on from there, and hang around taking pictures till the next train comes. This is more a tourist trip than a railfan trip.

Bern	leave	0822		SBB (S310, C560)
Interlaken West	leave	0912	0923	BLS (S310, C560)
Interlaken Ost	arrive	0915	0926	
Interlaken Ost	leave	0932		BOB (S311, C564)
Lauterbrunnen	arrive	0954		

Lauterbrunnen	leave	1010		WAB (S311, C564)
Kleine Scheidegg	arrive	1055		
Kleine Scheidegg	leave	1102		JB (S311, C564)
Jungfraujoch	arrive	1153		
Jungfraujoch	leave	1300		JB (S312, C564)
Kleine Scheidegg	arrive	1349		
Kleine Scheidegg	leave	1400		WAB (S312, C564)
Grindelwald	arrive	1445		
Grindelwald	leave	1450		BOB (S312, C564)
Interlaken Ost	arrive	1527		
Interlaken Ost	leave	1534	1545	BLS (S310, C560)
Interlaken West	arrive	1537	1550	
Bern	arrive		1638	

Interlaken Ost to Lauterbrunnen

Distance: 12 km
Company: Berner Oberland-Bahnen (BOB)
Track gauge: 1 meter
Maximum grade: 90 per mill (rack)

Lauterbrunnen to Kleine Scheidegg

Distance: 11 km
Company: Wengernalpbahn (WAB)
Track gauge: 80 cm
Maximum grade: 250 per mill (rack)

Kleine Scheidegg to Jungfraujoch

Distance: 9 km
Company: Jungfraubahn (JB)
Maximum grade: 250 per mill (rack)

The BOB, WAB, and JB are under one management. In 21 miles they lift you 9,469 feet to Jungfraujoch, highest station in Europe (11,333 feet) and highest subway station in the world.

The three most prominent peaks of the Bernese Alps are the Eiger, the Mönch, and the Jungfrau (Ogre, Monk, and Maiden); Jungfraujoch is in the col between the Monch and the Jungfrau.

In the 1880s Interlaken was already an established resort. The view of the Jungfrau from the meadow in the center of the town was the initial attraction. All kinds of excursions were available toward the mountains, mostly in horse-drawn coaches. The mountains themselves were inaccessible to all but experienced mountain-climbers. It was an age of railways, and railways were proposed to the summit of the Jungfrau. There was, of course, much debate over whether this was a good idea, even before the proposals for railways were submitted.

The first proposal was for a series of five funiculars ascending the mountain from the valley beyond Lauterbrunnen. The next was for a series of four funiculars in tunnels, then there was one for a pneumatic tube device.

The BOB was completed in 1890 from Interlaken to Grindelwald and Lauterbrunnen along the valleys of the Black and White Lutschine rivers, which come together at Zweilütschinen. The WAB, the world's longest rack-only railway, was opened over Kleine Scheidegg pass between the two terminals of the BOB in 1893.

In the summer of 1893 Adolf Guyer proposed starting a railway to the summit of the Jungfrau not in the valley but at Kleine Scheidegg, the summit of the WAB, which had been opened earlier that year. He proposed a railway mostly in tunnel but with a series of stations that would serve as viewing balconies and allow the lower part of the line to be in service while the upper part was still under construction.

The first part of the line opened in 1898 with much ceremony shortly before Guyer died. Tunneling continued upward. The line reached Jungfraujoch, where a station and a hotel were constructed. That proved to be the end of the line. The difficulty in continuing to the summit of the Jungfrau was that there would be little space inside the point of the mountain.

Until the 1950s the Jungfrau Railway was operated in two stages. The lower half was pure cog rail operation, and the upper half was at least partly run on adhesion. The line operates on three-phase alternating current, so there are two wires overhead, and the rails constitute the third conductor. The motors run at a constant speed, and to allow higher train speed on the easier grades, there is a two-speed gearbox between the motors and the axles. Coming downhill, Jungfraubahn trains use regenerative braking, returning about half the power they used going up.

The train stops for sightseeing at the stations of Eigerwand and Eismeer (Ogre Wall and Ice Sea). The stops are heralded by a burst of Swiss folk music, then announcements in German, French, Italian, Spanish, English, and Japanese.

The Jungfraujoch complex includes several restaurants and snack bars, places you can go out onto the snow, a tunnel and an elevator to an observatory, and a hall of ice sculptures. The altitude of Jungfraujoch is 11,333 feet. The air is thin, so when you get off the train, take it slow and easy for a few minutes. I haven't yet seen anyone pass out nor a squad of medics come running with oxygen tanks. There are no toilets on WAB and JB trains. You'll find them at all the stations.

One of Wengernalpbahn's yellow-and-green cars stands in the station at Grindelwald on September 21, 1988.

Kleine Scheidegg to Grindelwald

Distance: 8 km
Company: Wengernalpbahn (WAB)
Track gauge: 80 cm
Maximum grade: 250 per mill (rack)

Grindelwald to Interlaken Ost

Distance: 19 km
Company: BOB
Track gauge: 1 meter
Maximum grade: 120 per mill (rack)

From Kleine Scheidegg you can return by a different route through Grindelwald. The train descends from Kleine Scheidegg along the base of the north wall of the Eiger to Grindelwald Grund, where it reverses and climbs up to Grindelwald to connect with the BOB. WAB has a wye for turning trains at Kleine Scheidegg, so trains can run with the motor car at the lower end. You'll note that on this ride that the three railways have three different combinations of gauge and type of rack.

LUZERN

Interlaken West	leave	0823	0912	BLS (S310, C560)
Interlaken Ost	arrive	0826	0915	
Interlaken Ost	leave	0858	0919	SBB (S470, C561)
Brienz	arrive	0919	0938	
Luzern	arrive	1105	1105	
Luzern	leave	1654		
Brienz	leave	1822		
Interlaken Ost	arrive	1840		
Interlaken Ost	leave	1845		
Interlaken West	arrive	1848		

The 0912 train from Interlaken Ost operates from the beginning of June to late October. The 0858 operates the rest of the year.

Interlaken Ost to Luzern

Distance: 74 km
Company: SBB
Track gauge: 1 meter
Maximum grade: 120 per mill (rack)

The Brünig line is Swiss Federal's only meter-gauge line and its only line that uses rack assistance. It was opened in 1888 as part of the Bernese-Jura Railway and later became part of the Jura-Simplon system. The line was electrified in 1941 and 1942.

From Interlaken to Brienz the line follows the shore of the Brienzersee (Lake Brienz). From Brienz you can ride the Brienz Rothorn Bahn, a rack railway that still operates steam locomotives. At Meiringen the train reverses and in 3.3 miles climbs 1,335 feet out of the valley of the Aare to the summit of Brünig Pass. From there it descends into the upper basin of the Aa Valley (think how much better you'll be at crossword puzzles) to Giswil.

It's easier running from Giswil to Luzern. The train pauses at Alpnachstad, the lower terminal of the Pilatus Railway, steepest of the mountain railways (480 per mill); and at Hergiswil, the junction with the Luzern-Stans-Engelberg line.

Two Luzern–Interlaken trains each way carry a glass-topped

Panorama car offering meal service. Reservations are recommended. On weekends during summer and early fall an open air train called the ChäChä runs between Brünig Hasliberg, the summit of the pass, and Giswil. Reservations are necessary. Steam operates several times during late summer under the aegis of the Ballenberg Dampfbahn. For information, phone 41-33-982 80 80 or fax a request to 41-33-971-61-78.

MÜRREN AND SCHILTHORN

Go to Lauterbrunnen (the name means "pure fountain" — there's a waterfall that comes over the cliff there). Walk through the underground passage and board the funicular to Grutschalp. At the top board the meter gauge train to Mürren. The funicular runs at least twice an hour to connect with trains to and from Interlaken, and the Bergbahn Lauterbrunnen-Mürren (BLM) connects with all those trips (tables S313 and C564). The Swiss Pass is good for passage on the funicular and the train at the top. The BOB runs both the funicular and the train, though the cars are lettered BLM. The BLM is 4 kilometers long and has a maximum grade of 50 per mill.

A British book notes that the funicular and the BLM are both meter gauge so transfer of equipment is theoretically possible, though it must be fraught with difficulties. That indeed is how the BLM cars got up there.

Walk through the village of Mürren to the terminal of the cable line that will take you up to the Schilthorn (table S2460). This is the conveyance you see on all the travel posters, hanging from tiny little wires and you wouldn't go up in one of those if they paid you. All the others in the group were going, so I did too. My fears vanished, and I enjoyed the ride and the view.

At the summit you can have coffee or lunch with a stunning view. If you decide to wait till later, you'll have a better chance of finding lunch in Mürren than in Lauterbrunnen.

Prices for this line are not quoted in the current Swiss timetable. Several years ago the round trip fare was 52 francs; the Swiss Pass knocked it down to about 36 francs.

LAUSANNE

Lausanne spreads over several hills and ravines above Lac Léman. It is an important node in the SBB system, so the station is a busy one. My sole visit there, in 1987, was memorable for several things: rain, dinner at an excellent Tunisian restaurant, an incredible laundry bill at the hotel, and a tour guide who, as the bus passed through the zoo, pointed out the reptile house, which contained snacks and crocodiles. (Recently an Austrian bartender told me he didn't serve full meals, only snakes.)

HOTELS
• Hotel Continental (∗∗∗∗), 2 place de la Gare, CH-1001 Lausanne. Phone 41-21-320 15 51, fax 323 76 79. Single with bath, 140-195 francs; double with bath, 190-265 francs.
• Hotel Victoria (∗∗∗∗), 46 avenue de la Gare, CH-1001 Lausanne. Phone 41-21-320 57 71, fax 320 57 74. Single with bath, 165-195 francs; double with bath, 220-265 francs (rates are for May-October, except early July to mid-August, when the rates are lower). The hotel is opposite the uphill side of the station.

Lausanne is a convention and festival center, and the hotels have high-rate and low-rate seasons. There are a number of lower-priced hotels, but none appear to be near the station. Consider staying in Vevey, Montreux, or Morges:
• Hotel de la Couronne (∗∗∗), Grand-Rue 88, CH-1110 Morges. Phone 41-21-801 40 40, fax 802 12 97. Single with bath, 88-118 francs; double with bath, 138-168 francs. I have not stayed there, but as this book goes to press I am about to.

RECOMMENDED TRIPS
Bercher
Lausanne-Ouchy
Lausanne-Renens
Morges-Bière
Nyon-La Cure
Rhone Valley
Yverdon–Ste-Croix

BERCHER
A meter gauge line, the Lausanne-Echallens-Bercher (table S101), arrives and departs from a station beyond the commercial part of the city. In 1987 the station building at Lausanne-Chauderon looked like something you'd find on a rural branch of a bankrupt Midwestern railroad — definitely not Swiss-look-

ing, but it was scheduled for modernization as part of a project to widen avenue d'Echallens and create a private right of way for LEB. The railway was the first narrow gauge line in Switzerland. It was opened in 1873 and 1874, and electric operation began January 1, 1936 (steam operates on some summer Sundays). The line has been isolated since the closing of the Lausanne Tramways line to Renens in 1970. Trains run half-hourly as far as Echallens, 14 kilometers, and hourly beyond there to Bercher, 23 kilometers from Lausanne (table S101).

LAUSANNE–OUCHY

Lausanne has a rack-operated subway from Ouchy, down at lake level, up to a terminal named Flon across a viaduct from the commercial part of the city, with a stop at the main station. The ride takes 6 minutes. The line is only 1,485 meters long (4,871 feet); from Ouchy to Flon it climbs 104 meters (341 feet).

Below the SBB station the line is on the surface and you can walk along and over it and take pictures. One of the parallel streets is named Rue Funiculaire, which may say something about earlier technology on the line. Between the SBB station and Flon a second track parallels the Lausanne-Ouchy line. It seems to be separate operationally. See tables S103 and S104.

LAUSANNE–RENENS

A tramway line opened recently between Lausanne-Flon, at the top of the subway line mentioned above, and the suburb of Renens. The tram runs every 10 minutes weekdays, every 12 on Saturdays, and every 20 on Sundays; running time is 18 or 19 minutes (table S102). SBB-CFF service between Lausanne and Renens is shown in table S202: several trains per hour, running time 4 or 5 minutes, no intermediate stops. The subway runs frequently between the main station and Flon (tables S103 and S104), or you can walk — it's less than a quarter mile.

MORGES–BIÈRE

Genève	leave	0939	SBB (S150, C505)
Morges	arrive	0949	
Morges	leave	0953	BAM (S156, C502)
Bière	arrive	1021	
Bière	leave	1048	
Morges	arrive	1118	
Morges	leave	1137	
Genève	arrive	1153	

For route information see page 87.

NYON–LA CURE

Genève	leave	0903	SBB (S150, C505)
Nyon	arrive	0926	
Nyon	leave	0935	NStCM (S155, C501)
La Cure	arrive	1022	
La Cure	leave	1035	
Nyon	arrive	1123	
Nyon	leave	1132	
Genève	arrive	1157	

For route information see page 88.

RHÔNE VALLEY

The excursions described from Montreux, Aigle, Bex, and Martigny can be made easily from Lausanne. Departure times for Lausanne are shown in the Rhône Valley section. See pages 122-129.

YVERDON–STE-CROIX

Lausanne	leave	0910	SBB (S210, C500)
Yverdon	arrive	0933	
Yverdon	leave	0946	YSteC (S212)
Ste-Croix	arrive	1023	
Ste-Croix	leave	1034	
Yverdon	arrive	1112	
Yverdon	leave	1126	
Lausanne	arrive	1150	

Distance: 24 km
Company: Yverdon–Ste-Croix
Track gauge: 1 meter
Maximum grade: 44 per mill

The Yverdon-Ste. Croix was opened in 1893 and operated by the Jura-Simplon Railway until 1897, when the YSteC took over its own operation. Until 1945, when it was electrified using the 15,000-volt system of SBB, it was noted for a roster of Mallet-type locomotives, three of them from the Rhätische Bahn.

The line ascends through wooded country from an elevation of 435 meters at Yverdon to 1,066 meters at Ste-Croix. The lower part of the line offers views across fields to villages with the Jura ridge beyond. Most of the climb occurs above Baulmes. At Six-Fontaines, where there is a chalet-style station, the line makes a horseshoe turn, then passes through five tunnels. There are occasional views through the trees, then a short passage through a gorge.

LUGANO

My feelings about Lugano are mixed, but I like it more each time. It is in a gorgeous setting on a lake, but it's a crowded, noisy place, far more Italian in character than Swiss. That may be why people go there. SBB's line runs along the side of a hill above the city; a funicular runs from the station down to the center of the city.

HOTELS

The Hotel Cristallo (***), much recommended by the rail travel press, is right at the bottom of the funicular, at Piazza Cioccaro 9, CH-6900 Lugano. It is not listed in the current *Swiss Hotel Guide*. Its rates were considerably lower than those of its neighbors. I have selected three hotels from the guide simply by address.

• Colorado (***), Via Maraini 19, CH-6907 Lugano, phone 41-91-994 16 31, fax 993 12 66. Single with bath, 120-150 francs; double with bath, 160-210 francs. It is two or three blocks south of the station, on the hillside above the city.

• Lugano-Dante (****), Piazza Cioccaro 5, CH-6900 Lugano, phone 41-91-910 57 00, fax 910 57 77. Single with bath, 150-200 francs; double with bath, 230-300 francs.

• Romantik Hotel Ticino (****), Piazza Cioccaro 1, CH-6901 Lugano, phone 41-91-922 77 72, fax 923 62 78. Single with bath, 240-300 francs; double with bath, 340-420 francs.

Obviously the word "Romantik" costs you something, (and often one of its meanings is "the floors aren't level"). Consider instead:

• Hotel de la Paix (****), Via Cattori 18, CH-6902 Lugano, phone 41-91-994 23 32, fax 994 95 18. Single with bath 190-230 francs; double with bath, 270-320 francs. I have stayed there several times with tour groups. The attached semi-outdoor restaurant serves the best pizza south of Bex. The hotel is south of the main station, maybe a mile — with luggage, take a taxi. It is much closer to the Lugano-Paradiso station, the first station south of the main station, but still not walking distance with luggage.

FUNICULARS

In addition to the funicular from the station down to the center of Lugano there are two others. One runs up Monte San Salvatore from Lugano-Paradiso. It is possible to get pictures of the funicular crossing above SBB trains at Lugano-Paradiso. Schedules are in table S2652. Price was 14 francs round trip a few years ago. The operation is unusual. Instead of two cars that run the full length, passing in the middle, the two cars balance each other but run on only the lower half or the upper half of the line, and passengers change cars at the midpoint. At the top of the mountain is a little chapel with a spectacular view from the roof, reached by a vertigo-inducing stairway.

The other funicular is up Monte Brè from Cassarate (table S2653). You can see its route if you look east across the city from the SBB station. Price is 15 francs round trip. Trolley bus route 1 gets you from the center of Lugano to Cassarate.

RAILWAY COMPANIES IN ADDITION TO SBB
Ferrovia Lugano-Ponte Tresa (FLP)

RECOMMENDED TRIPS
Locarno and Domodossola
Monte Generoso
Ponte Tresa
Swiss Miniatur at Melide

LOCARNO AND DOMODOSSOLA

Lugano	leave	0857	SBB S600, C550)
Bellinzona	arrive	0923	
Bellinzona	leave	0938	SBB (S630, C548)
Locarno	arrive	0959	
Locarno	leave	1035	FART (S620, C549)
Domodossola	arrive	1214	
Domodossola	leave	1444	
Locarno	arrive	1625	
Locarno	leave	1630	
Bellinzona	arrive	1653	
Bellinzona	leave	1657	
Lugano	arrive	1723	

The major points of this route are described in the section on Brig. Locarno is a very pretty town and to me more pleasant than Lugano. You could make an entire circle through Domodossola, Brig, Andermatt, and Göschenen, but it wouldn't make much sense to do it from Lugano — you'd duplicate much of your ride to and from Lugano.

MONTE GENEROSO

Lugano	leave	0952	SBB (S60, C550)
Capolago	arrive	1006	
Capolago	leave	1018	MG (S636)
Generoso Vetta	arrive	1055	
Generoso Vetta	leave	1200	
Capolago	arrive	1240	
Capolago	leave	1316	
Lugano	arrive	1334	

Capolago-Generoso

Distance: 9 km

Company: Ferrovia del Monte Generoso (MG)

Maximum grade: 220 per mill (rack)

I have not ridden the Monte Generoso railway. About the only data I can give you is the track gauge, 80 centimeters.

PONTE TRESA

Distance: 12 km

Company: Ferrovia Lugano-Ponte Tresa (FLP)

Maximum grade: 30 per mill

Meter gauge FLP trains leave their station in Lugano, just across the street from the SBB station, every 20 minutes on weekdays and every 30 on weekends and holidays (table S635). The trip takes 21 minutes. The line goes past the Lugano airport and follows the shore of Lake Lugano to Ponte Tresa, on the Italian border.

SWISS MINIATUR

At Melide is a miniature city and garden railroad, 1:25 scale. It's worth seeing for the trains and also for the little lizards that inhabit the place, looking like scale model crocodiles. It is across the street from the SBB station at Melide, where the main line of the Gotthard Route crosses Lake Lugano on a causeway built on a glacial moraine. Admission is was 8 francs in 1991. Swiss Miniatur is open mid-March through October, 0830-1800.

Lugano	leave	0923	SBB (S600, C550)
Lugano-Paradiso	leave	0925	
Melide	arrive	0931	
Melide	leave	1126	
Lugano-Paradiso	arrive	1129	
Lugano	arrive	1134	

LUZERN

The French form of the name, Lucerne, is usually used in English, but I'll stick with the German, since that's the form used locally. There's lots of touristy stuff to do here, and your nonrail guidebook can tell you about it. Luzern is a good walking city. The older part of the city is north of the River Reuss, and if you go up the hill you'll get to the old city wall. You can walk along part of it and climb up in the towers, including one with a clock. The footbridges over the river are notable, too. The Chapel Bridge, the one you see in the pictures, burned in 1993 but has been replaced in kind. The lion monument — you've heard about that, too — is worth seeing. If you can look at it and not feel a surge of pity, you have more control than I.

The Swiss Transport Museum (Verkehrshaus) is worth at least a half day. Take a boat from the station quay or the route 2 trolley bus, or walk along the lakefront — it's maybe a mile. I have heard that the Swiss Pass yields a discount on the admission price. In one of the exhibit halls are several displays and video monitors to keep you apprised of trains on the Luzern–Arth-Goldau line, which passes the museum. A model railroad depicts part of the Gotthard route, a small theater lets you ride a train with the engineer, and a simulator lets you run a streetcar in Bern. It's worth taking a curve too fast to see what happens (I did it and survived).

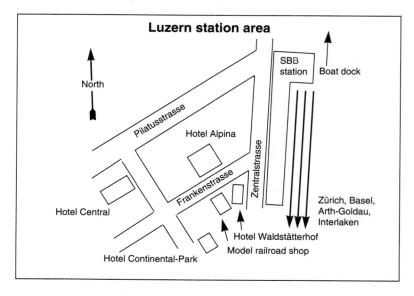

Luzern station area

Luzern's station was destroyed by fire in 1971. In the years thereafter numerous studies were undertaken while passengers and staff coped with temporary facilities. A new station of modern design opened on February 5, 1991, exactly 20 years after the disaster. Four of the station's 14 tracks are meter gauge for the trains of SBB's Brünig line and the Luzern-Stans-Engelberg Railway.

HOTELS

• Alpina (✳✳✳), Frankenstrasse 6, CH-6002 Luzern, phone 41-41-210 00 77, fax 210 89 44. Single with bath, 104-120 francs; double with bath, 1930235 francs. Walk down the platform toward the station, turn left at the end of the tracks, and go out to the street. Cross the street, turn left, and then take the first right. The Alpina is about halfway up the block. I chose the Alpina for its location in 1986 and it proved comfortable and friendly. I have stayed there several times since.

• Central (✳✳✳), Morgartenstrasse 4, CH-6002 Luzern; phone 41-41-210 50 60, fax 210 66 88. Single with bath, 115-158 francs; double with bath, 176-242 francs. Go to the corner beyond the Alpina, turn right, and cross the street. The Central is the former Continental, under new management. I stayed there several times before the change and considered it convenient and comfortable, even if the rooms were a little drab and a few were entered through their bathrooms (one of the problems of adding plumbing to an old building is that you can't always run the pipes where you want).

• Continental-Park (✳✳✳✳), Murbacherstrasse 4, CH-6002 Luzern; phone 41-41-228-90 50, fax 228 90 49. Single with bath, 180-230 francs; double with bath, 300-390 francs. The Park was affiliated with the Continental and, still under that management, has been upgraded and renovated. It is in essentially the same position on the street as the Alpina but one block south.

• Waldstätterhof (✳✳✳), Zentralstrasse 4, CH-6002; phone 41-41-23 54 93, fax 23 09 59. Single with bath, 115-125 francs; double with bath, 166-188 francs. The restaurant of the Waldstätterhof is an alcohol-free establishment — order a beer and you'll get a Clausthaler.

In that neighborhood you'll find several restaurants. A few blocks farther and toward the river is the Walliser Kanne, which is ethnic Swiss. There are more restaurants across the river. The ground-floor brasserie of the Schwanen restaurant is fine for lunch, as is the Stadtkeller; the Walliser Spycher on a side street in the old part of town is another good ethnic Swiss restaurant.

There is a coin-operated laundry, Jet Wasch, at Bruchstrasse 28. Follow Pilatusstrasse about 7 blocks west from the station, then turn right (north) on Bruchstrasse. The laundromat is about 3 blocks on your left. Across Frankenstrasse from the Hotel Alpina is a model railroad shop.

RAILWAY COMPANIES IN ADDITION TO SBB
Luzern-Stans-Engelberg (LSE) — meter gauge

RECOMMENDED TRIPS
Engelberg
Mount Pilatus
Mount Rigi

ENGELBERG

Luzern	leave	0913	LSE (S480, C552)
Engelberg	arrive	1012	
Engelberg	leave	1045	
Luzern	arrive	1145	

Distance: 33 km
Company: Luzern-Stans-Engelberg
Track gauge: 1 meter
Maximum grade: 246 per mill (rack)

For the first 8 kilometers bright red LSE trains follow the meter gauge tracks of SBB's Brünig line (described in the section on Interlaken). At Hergiswil the LSE branches left into a tunnel opened in 1964. Previously the first leg of a trip from Luzern to Engelberg was by boat to Stansstad. (It's still possible and pleasant — tables S3601 and C558.) The line follows a valley and climbs gently. Then at Obermatt pinions engage rack, and the train climbs steeply for the last few kilometers to Engelberg.

Engelberg is a resort town, both summer and winter. The Benedictine abbey has a church built in the 1730s that is worth a look. Turn left as you leave the station, then turn right and walk through the town. It's about 10 minutes' walk. If it's a good day, consider a cable car ride to the top of one of the mountains — tables S2530-S2538.

MOUNT PILATUS

Luzern	leave	0824	1024	SBB (S470, C561)
Alpnachstad	arrive	0840	1039	
Alpnachstad	leave	0850	1050	PB (S473, C551)
Pilatus-Kulm	arrive	0920	1120	

A Luzern-Stans-Engelberg train departs Engelberg with Mount Hahnen as a backdrop. LSE photo.

Pilatus-Kulm	leave	—	PB (S2517)
Fräkmüntegg	arrive	—	(6 minutes)
Fräkmüntegg	leave	—	PB (S2516)
Kriens	arrive	—	(31 minutes)
Kriens	leave	—	trolley bus, route 1
Luzern	arrive	—	

Luzern to Alpnachstad

Distance: 13 km

Company: SBB (meter gauge)

Maximum grade: 20 per mill

The Brünig line follows the Vierwaldstätter See and the Alpnacher See as far as Alpnachstad.

Alpnachstad to Pilatus Kulm

Distance: 4.4 km

Company: Pilatusbahn (PB)

Maximum grade: 480 per mill (rack)

This is the steepest rack railway in the world. It uses the Locher system, which has notches cut into the sides of the head of the rack rail and a pair of pinions mounted horizontally under the car — a bit like the gearing of an eggbeater.

You can descend by the same route, or you can take a series of aerial cable lines through Fräkmüntegg to Kriens. A 5-minute walk at Kriens takes you to the route 1 trolley bus, which will carry you back to the station.

The round-trip fare from Alpnachstad to the summit of Pilatus and the fare from Alpnachstad over the top to Kriens are both 58 francs. I don't know whether the Swiss Pass yields a discount, but it won't hurt to ask. The cog railway is closed in the winter, but the cable cars run year round.

MOUNT RIGI

Luzern	leave	0900	boat (S3600, C557)
Vitznau	arrive	0957	
Vitznau	leave	1010	RB (S603, C551)
Rigi-Kulm	arrive	1040	
Rigi-Kulm	leave	1104	RB (S602, C551)
Arth-Goldau	arrive	1147	
Arth-Goldau	leave	1213	SBB (S600, C550)
Luzern	arrive	1243	

Vitznau to Luzern

The dock in Luzern is across the plaza from the station. Most trips stop at the Transportation Museum 10 minutes after departing Luzern. The Swiss Pass is good for passage on the boat. Most boats have snack bars; some have restaurants. A few schedules are operated with side-wheel steamers.

Vitznau to Rigi-Kulm

Distance: 7 km
Company: Rigi Bahnen (RB)
Maximum grade: 250 per mill (R)

The Vitznau-Rigi Bahn was the first cog railway in Switzerland. On August 12, 1863, Niklaus Riggenbach, Locomotive Engineer (Chief Mechanical Officer) of the Central Railway of Switzerland, patented a rack-and-pinion railway. Riggenbach visited the Mount Washington Cog Railway in New Hampshire soon after it opened in 1869. On his return he cast around for a suitable mountain to try his ideas.

He chose Mount Rigi, noted for the views from its summit. Construction began in 1869 and the line reached Staffelhöhe and opened in May 1871. Staffelhöhe was as far as the line could go within the Canton of Luzern; the Canton of Schwyz, which included the summit, wanted to build its own line from Arth-Goldau to the summit.

The rivalry calmed down when the federal government assumed the authority to issue all railway charters. The Schwyz company opened a line from Staffelhöhe to the summit, Rigi-Kulm, for the VRB in 1873. The Arth-Rigi-Bahn from Arth-

Goldau to the summit opened in 1875; the two lines are parallel from Staffelhöhe to the summit. The VRB was electrified in 1937; the ARB was electrified in 1907.

You'll have to buy a ticket at Vitznau. The round-trip fare to the summit is 54 francs, as is the through rate, up one side and down the other. The Swiss Pass reduces the price to 41 francs.

You'll note that part of the plaza between the boat dock and the Vitznau station is a covered turntable pit. You may see a steam locomotive sitting in the engine house there.

During the summer of 1997 in celebration of the 150th anniversary of Swiss railroads the 0911 departure from Arth-Goldau and the 1440 departure from Rigi Kulm were steam-powered. In addition steam-powered trains operated between Rigi Staffel and Rigi Kulm. The steam locomotives still get out occasionally — watch for posters in the stations and check the footnotes in the Official Timetable.

Rigi-Kulm to Arth-Goldau

Distance: 9 km
Company: Arth-Rigi-Bahn (ARB)
Maximum grade: 201 per mill (R)

At the summit you can usually find the cars of both lines. The line starts down parallel to the Vitznau line, but soon the Arth line is deep in forest. The ARB, the VRB, the Rorschach-Heiden-Bergbahn, and the Lausanne-Ouchy lines are the only standard-gauge rack lines in Switzerland.

Arth-Goldau to Luzern

Distance: 28 km
Company: SBB
Maximum grade: 11 per mill

The Luzern and Zürich lines of the Gotthard route join at Arth-Goldau. The station serves two towns, Arth, on the shore of the Zuger See, and Goldau, inland where the station is. The ARB platform is upstairs crosswise to the platform for the Luzern line, which is part of the main north-south freight route. The station also serves the Südostbahn, which runs over the mountains to Pfäffikon and Rapperswil.

From Arth-Goldau the train follows the shore of the Zuger See (Lake Zug) for a short distance, then diverges from the freight line to follow the shore of the Vierwaldstätter See (Lake of the Four Woodland Cantons). You'll have good views of Mount Rigi. Just beyond the Swiss Transport Museum the train swings into a tunnel. The train will make almost a complete circle before it reaches the station in Luzern.

THE RHÔNE VALLEY

AIGLE

Aigle is a small town whose principal business is winemaking. On the outskirts of town — within walking distance — is a chateau containing a winemaking museum.

• Hotel du Nord (✳✳✳), 4 rue Colomb, CH-1860 Aigle, phone 41-25-26 10 55, fax 26 42 48. Single with bath, 105 francs; without bath, 95 francs; double with bath, 170 francs; without bath, 130 francs.

It's about a 5-minute walk from the station. Come out of the station and keep walking in the same direction, following the tracks of the Aigle-Leysin Railway up toward the center of the town. The hotel is on the right just after the street starts a bend to the right. You'll find an elegant dining room upstairs and a brasserie (grillroom) at street level. A block or two to the south is the Cafe du Marché, which offered a good fondue in 1986.

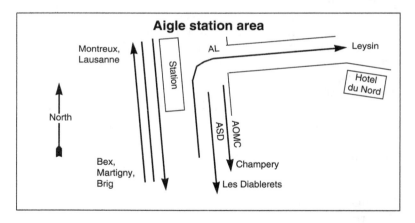

MARTIGNY

Martigny (Octodurum in Roman times) is located at the right-angle bend in the valley. It is the jumping-off point for the line to Chamonix and also the Martigny-Orsières Railway, which I have not ridden yet. Directly across from the station is the

• Hotel Forclaz-Touring (✳✳✳), 15 rue du Léman, CH-1920 Martigny, phone 41-26-22 27 01, fax 22 41 79. Single with bath, 85-120 francs; double with bath, 125-170 francs.

MONTREUX

You might find Montreux a livelier place. It is a resort and convention city, so you may not be able to get a hotel room on the spur of the moment. Two stations south of Montreux on the shore of Lac Léman is the castle of Chillon. It's worth seeing.

• Hotel Terminus (∗∗∗) is just up the the hill from the station at 22 Avenue de la Gare, CH-1820 Montreux; Phone 41-21-963 12 31, fax 963 55 67. Single with bath, 120-160 francs; double with bath, 160-210 francs.

VEVEY

The next major town toward Lausanne from Montreux is Vevey, a pleasant manufacturing town.

• Hotel Pavillon et Residence (∗∗∗∗), Place de la Gare, CH-1800 Vevey, phone 41-21-923 61 61, fax 921 14 77. Single with bath, 170-270 francs; double with bath, 220-320 francs. It is directly opposite the entrance of the SBB station.

• Hotel De Famille (∗∗∗), Place de la Gare, phone 41-21-921 39 31, fax 921 43 47. Single with bath, 95-125 francs; without bath, 70-90 francs; double with bath, 150-210 francs; without bath, 120-150 francs. It is just south of the station.

RAILWAY COMPANIES IN ADDITION TO SBB

At Aigle:

Aigle-Leysin (AL)

Aigle-Sépey-Diablerets (ASD)

Aigle-Ollon-Monthey-Champéry (AOMC)

All three are meter gauge lines operated by Transports Publics du Chablais. You can easily ride all three in one day, including stops to eat lunch and admire the views.

At Bex:

Bex-Villars-Bretaye (BVB), meter gauge, also operated by Transports Publics du Chablais. The company also runs a streetcar from station to the center of Bex.

At Martigny:

Martigny-Chatelard (MC), meter gauge

Martigny-Orsières (MO), standard gauge

At Montreux:

Montreux-Oberland Bernois (MOB), meter gauge and the steepest adhesion railway in Switzerland as it climbs away from the lake. At Chamby it connects with the Blonay-Chamby, a museum railroad.

Montreux-Glion (MGl) and Glion–Rochers-de-Naye (GN), both 80-centimeter gauge and part of the MOB family.

At Vevey:

Chemins de fer Électriques Veveysans (CEV), meter gauge and rack-operated above Blonay, where it connects with the Blonay-Chamby, a museum railroad.

RECOMMENDED TRIPS

Chamonix
Champéry
Les Diablerets
Leysin
Puidoux-Chexbres
Villars and Bretaye
Zweisimmen, Interlaken, and Luzern

CHAMONIX

Genève	leave	0840	SBB (S150, C505)
Lausanne	leave	0929	SBB (S100, C570)
Vevey	leave	0943	
Montreux	leave	0950	
Aigle	leave	1000	
Martigny	arrive	1021	
Martigny	leave	1043	MC (S132, C572)
Le Châtelard–Frontière	arrive	1131	
Le Châtelard–Frontière	leave	1136	SNCF (S5120, C572)
Chamonix	arrive	1213	
Chamonix	leave	1304	1510
Le Châtelard–Frontière	arrive	1343	1547
Le Châtelard–Frontière	leave	1347	1553
Martigny	arrive	1439	1644
Martigny	leave	1507	1707
Aigle	arrive	1524	1724
Montreux	arrive	1533	1733
Vevey	arrive	1542	1742
Lausanne	arrive	1556	1756
Genève	arrive	1642	1842

Schedules on the Martigny–Vallorcine–Chamonix route are an exception to the hourly intervals found nearly everywhere else.

Martigny to Vallorcine

Distance: 21 km
Company: Martigny-Châtelard (MC)
Maximum grade: 200 per mill (rack)

This line is one of the most scenic in Europe. From Martigny, which is located at the right-angle bend in the Rhône Valley, the meter gauge MC follows the Rhône northwest downstream to

Vernayaz. There it makes a hairpin turn in a tunnel and turns southwest to follow the Trient gorge to the French border at Le Châtelard. Trains draw power from overhead wires as far as Vernayaz, then use third rail to Vallorcine.

From June to October you can make a side trip from Le Châtelard to a dam (the French word is "barrage") above Emosson. To do so, you have to travel by funicular, a 60-cm gauge railway, and a cog monorail, which I'd have to see to believe. See table S2143.

MC's trains connect at Vallorcine, Le Châtelard–Frontière, or Le Châtelard–Giétroz with a meter-gauge line of French National Railways. It is possible to go from Chamonix to Genève (Eaux-Vives station, across the river from the main station, on tram line 12) or to Evian-les-Bains, then by boat across Lac Léman to Lausanne (tables S5120, S5110, S3152, C367, C368, and C372). It will take you most of a day and is probably easier than the number of timetables would imply.

Vallorcine to Chamonix
Company: Société Nationale des Chemins de fer Francais

French National Railways' Savoie line from St. Gervais to Vallorcine was built by the Paris-Lyon-Mediterranée. It was opened as far as Chamonix in 1902 and extended to a connection with the Martigny-Châtelard in 1908. Like the MC it is meter gauge and electrified with third rail. In 1958 the line became passenger-only.

CHAMPÉRY

Genève	leave	0818	SBB (S150, C505)
Lausanne	leave	0904	SBB (S100, C570)
Vevey	leave	0918	
Montreux	leave	0925	
Aigle	arrive	0934	
Martigny	leave	0907	SBB (S100, C570)
Aigle	arrive	0924	
Aigle	leave	0940	AOMC (S126, C571)
Champéry	arrive	1044	
Champéry	leave	1106	
Aigle	arrive	1210	

Aigle to Champéry
Distance: 23 km
Company: Aigle-Ollon-Monthey-Champéry (AOMC)
Track gauge: 1 meter
Maximum grade: 135 per mill (rack)

The AOMC was built by two separate companies. It opened

in 1907 from Aigle to Monthey and in 1908 from Monthey to Champéry. The two companies joined in 1946.

The line goes southeast from Aigle to Ollon, then crosses SBB's Rhône Valley main line and St. Maurice-St. Gingolph branch before arriving at Monthey, on the left bank of the Rhône. The station is worthy of any of the U. S.'s new light-rail systems. Trains reverse there and may cut off and add trailers, or trailers may go through and motors not. Be alert.

From Monthey the line follows the Val d'Illiez up to Champéry. There are three stretches of rack operation. The porcelain-footprints-and-hole john in the Champéry station is worth a look.

LES DIABLERETS

Genève	leave	0818	SBB (S150, C505)
Lausanne	leave	0904	SBB (S100, C570)
Vevey	leave	0918	
Montreux	leave	0925	
Aigle	arrive	0934	
Martigny	leave	0907	SBB (S100, C570)
Aigle	arrive	0924	
Aigle	leave	0941	ASD (S124, C571))
Les Diablerets	arrive	1025	
Les Diablerets	leave	1058	
Aigle	arrive	1151	

Aigle to Les Diablerets

Distance: 23 km
Company: Aigle-Sépey-Diablerets (ASD)
Track gauge: 1 meter
Maximum grade: 60 per mill

The ASD was opened in 1913 and until recently used its original equipment, partly because the line had been operating under threat of closure for a number of years. The line's future has been assured now by assistance from the canton; track repair is under way, and new cars are in service.

The line crosses the AOMC almost immediately after leaving the Aigle station, follows city streets for a way, then passes the chateau and begins to climb. There are good views back toward the chateau and the town. The track sticks to the south side of the valley except for a quick trip on a handsome concrete arch bridge across the Grande Eau to Le Sépey, where the train reverses direction (not all trains go to Le Sepéy; some reverse at Les Planches and have a connecting bus). The 0941 from Aigle carries an open car in good weather on summer weekends.

Left to right, Aigle-Leysin, Aigle-Sépey-Diablerets, and Aigle-Ollon-Monthey-Champéry cars stand in the station plaza at Aigle in March 1994.

Except in winter, five postal buses a day run between Les Diablerets and Gstaad, on the MOB between Montreux and Zweisimmen (table S120.15). In summer there are three bus trips a day between Les Diablerets and Villars (table S127.15).

LEYSIN

Genève	leave	0818	SBB (S150, C505)
Lausanne	leave	0904	SBB (S100, C570)
Vevey	leave	0918	
Montreux	leave	0925	
Aigle	arrive	0934	
Martigny	leave	0907	SBB (S100, C570)
Aigle	arrive	0924	
Aigle	leave	0940	AL (S125, C571))
Leysin–Grand Hôtel	arrive	1012	
Leysin–Grand Hôtel	leave	1035	
Aigle	arrive	1118	

Aigle to Leysin

Distance: 6 km
Company: Aigle-Leysin (AL)
Track gauge: 1 meter
Maximum grade: 230 per mill (rack)

The AL, opened in 1900, is the oldest of the meter gauge lines in Aigle. The line runs through streets on adhesion, reverses at the carbarn, then climbs to Leysin with rack assistance.

PUIDOUX–CHEXBRES

An SBB line runs between Vevey and Puidoux-Chexbres (table S111). It climbs from 386 meters at Vevey to 618 meters at Puidoux-Chexbres, 232 meters in 8 kilometers with a maxium grade of 40 per mill. The line offers views out over the lake. Trains leave Vevey at 10 past each hour and arrive Puidoux-Chexbres at 22 past; they return at 36 past, arriving Vevey at 48 past. There are immediate connections with local trains to and from Lausanne and Fribourg (table S250) at Puidoux-Chexbres.

VILLARS AND BRETAYE

Genève	leave	0840	SBB (S150, C505)	
Lausanne	leave	0929	SBB (S100, C570)	
Vevey	leave	0943		
Montreux	leave	0950		
Aigle	leave	1000		
Bex	arrive	1006		
Martigny	leave	0931	SBB (S100, C570)	
Bex	arrive	0946		
Bex	leave	1009	BVB (S127, C571)	
Villars	arrive	1051		
Villars	leave	1100	BVB (S128)	
Col-de-Bretaye	arrive	1120		
Col-de-Bretaye	leave	1125		
Villars	arrive	1145		
Villars	leave	1253	1104	
Bex	arrive	1337	1148	

Bex to Villars
Distance: 12 km
Company: Bex-Villars-Bretaye (BVB)
Track gauge: 1 meter
Maximum grade: 195 per mill (rack)

Villars to Col-de-Bretaye
Distance: 5 km
Company: Bex-Villars-Bretaye (BVB)
Track gauge: 1 meter
Maximum grade: 170 per mill (rack)

The line runs in streets from the SBB station through Bex to Bévieux, where the carbarn is located. Then it climbs steeply through forest on rack for a while before resuming adhesion running along the side of the road into Villars, a ski resort. It's a pretty ride. BVB also runs local streetcar service on the same tracks between Bex and Bévieux, 3 kilometers (table S129). The line's shops are at Bévieux.

The Villars–Col-de-Bretaye line doesn't appear on the Swiss Holiday Card schematic map, not even for reduced fare upon presentation of card. It costs SFr 21.60 round trip. Train operation depends on weather and snow conditions.

Several years ago a reader of this guide wrote specifically to recommend the pizza at the Buffet de la Gare, the Bex station restaurant. I've since checked it out myself. Five stars. Worth the trip (except on Mondays, when it's closed).

ZWEISIMMEN, INTERLAKEN, LUZERN, AND BRIG

Genève	leave	0740		SBB (S150, C505)
Lausanne	arrive	0821		
Lausanne	leave	0829		SBB (S100, C570)
Vevey	leave	0843		
Montreux	arrive	0848		
Martigny	leave	0807		SBB (S100, C570)
Aigle	leave	0824		
Montreux	arrive	0833		
Montreux	leave	0902		MOB (S120, C566)
Zweisimmen	arrive	1058		Change trains
On to Interlaken and Luzern				
Zweisimmen	leave	1105		SEZ (S320, C565)
Spiez	arrive	1151		
Spiez	leave	1206		BLS (S310, C560)
Interlaken Ost	arrive	1226		
Interlaken Ost	leave	1300		SBB (S470, C561)
Luzern	arrive	1505		
Back to Montreux via Brig				
Zweisimmen	leave	1105		SEZ (S320, C565)
Spiez	arrive	1151		
Spiez	leave	1158		BLS (S300, C560)
Brig	arrive	1303		
Brig	leave	1336		SBB (S100, C570)
Martigny	arrive	1437		
Aigle	arrive	1459		
Montreux	arrive	1508		
Vevey	arrive	1517		
Lausanne	arrive	1531		
Lausanne	leave	1539		
Genève	arrive	1620		
Same route back to Montreux				
Zweisimmen	leave	1200	1244	
Montreux	arrive	1400	1428	

Montreux	leave	1425	1450
Aigle	arrive	1435	1500
Martigny	arrive	1522	1553
Montreux	leave	1410	1435
Vevey	arrive	1416	1441
Lausanne	arrive	1431	1456
Genève	arrive	1520	1542

Montreux to Zweisimmen

Distance: 62 km
Company: Montreux-Oberland Bernois (MOB)
Track gauge: 1 meter
Maximum grade: 73 per mill

The MOB connects two of Switzerland's principal tourist areas — Lac Léman (Lake Geneva) and the Bernese Oberland. There have been proposals for years to standard-gauge the MOB and SBB's Brünig line between Luzern and Interlaken to allow through service, and recently there has been another, less expensive proposal — to add a third rail for meter-gauge trains between Zweisimmen and Interlaken Ost.

The MOB was the first narrow-gauge line in Switzerland to offer dining cars, and in summer 1931 the Wagons-Lits company operated a train of Pullmans (which in Europe are luxurious daytime cars, not sleepers), the Golden Mountain Express, over the line. In 1979 MOB introduced air-conditioned, glass-roofed cars for the Panoramic Express, and even more recently a Crystal Panoramic with a front end observation car. The new cars seat first-class passengers two-by-two in cars with non-opening windows. You may find the older cars with openable windows and two-and-one seating in first class more pleasant riding and less crowded — the tourists flock to the new cars. I have cited schedules for the ordinary trains.

The MOB has a branch from Zweisimmen to Lenk and operates two other railways that form a line out of Montreux, the Montreux-Glion and the Glion–Rochers-de-Naye (table S121). Rochers-de-Naye is at an elevation of 1,970 meters, with a good view. The company recently received a steam locomotive from the Swiss Locomotive & Machine Works in Winterthur.

The MOB line has a 73 per mill grade as it climbs away from Lac Léman, from Montreux at 395 meters to Jor at 1,080 meters — 2,246 feet in 11 miles, which amounts to an average of 4 percent. The climb takes a lot of twisting and turning. At Chamby you can connect with the streetcars and steam-powered trains of the Blonay-Chamby museum line, which operates on weekends June through October (table S105). At the other end the BC connects with the Chemins de fer Électriques Veveysans (table S112), which can get you from Blonay back down to the SBB at Vevey or up to Les Pléiades.

East of the summit the MOB follows valleys down through Montbovon (where it connects with the Gruyères-Fribourg-Morat — also known as the Chemin de fer Fribourgeois), Château d'Oex, and Gstaad, a world-famed winter resort. As the train approaches Zweisimmen you get a view of the station below, then the train enters a horseshoe tunnel and descends to the floor of the valley.

From Zweisimmen you can continue to Spiez, using the standard gauge Spiez-Erlenbach-Zweisimmen; from Spiez to Interlaken Ost on the BLS; and from Interlaken Ost (East) to Luzern on SBB's meter-gauge Brünig line. At Spiez you can turn south to ride the Bern-Lötschberg-Simplon to Brig and a connection with SBB's Rhône Valley main line (the route is described in the section on Brig).

Zweisimmen to Spiez

Distance: 35 km
Company: Spiez-Erlenbach-Zweisimmen (SEZ)
Maximum grade: 25 per mill

The line, known as the Simmentalbahn, follows the deep valley of the Simme River down to Spiez on the shore of the Thuner See (Lake of Thun). The SEZ is one of the BLS group of railways; the shops are at Spiez.

Spiez to Interlaken

Distance: 18 km
Company: Bern-Lötschberg-Simplon (BLS)
Maximum grade: 15 per mill (descending)

From Spiez to Interlaken the BLS runs along the shore of the Thuner See. Five minutes before Interlaken Ost is the Interlaken West station, at the center of the town near most of the hotels. Interlaken Ost is the junction with SBB's meter gauge line over Brünig Pass to Luzern and with the Berner Oberland-Bahnen up to the Jungfrau region. For descriptions of the Brünig line and the Jungfrau lines see the section on Interlaken.

ST. GALLEN

St. Gallen (St-Gall in French) is the principal city of northeast Switzerland. Southeast of the station (the tracks in the station run more or less east and west) is the old part of town with narrow streets. It's a good place for your after-dinner walk. The cathedral is worth a look (it's closed to sightseers during worship services), and be sure to admire the roof of the St. Lawrence Church nearby. A few miles north of St. Gallen is the Bodensee (Lake Constance).

HOTELS
• Walhalla (∗∗∗∗), Bahnhofplatz, CH-9001 St. Gallen, phone 41-71-22 29 22, fax 22 29 66. Single with bath, 150-170 francs; double with bath, 230-250 francs.

As you come up from the tunnel under the tracks at the east end of the station the hotel is to your left and across the street. The hotel restaurant is quite good.
• Gallo (∗∗∗), St. Jakobstrasse 62, CH-9000 St. Gallen, phone 41-71-245 27 27, fax 245 45 93. Single with bath,150-160 francs; double with bath, 200-280 francs.

The Gallo is east of the center of the city, easily accessible by trolley bus (your Swiss Pass is valid on it). In the plaza in front of the station find a No. 3-Heiligkreuz trolley bus and ride to the OLMA stop (it's the fifth stop, I think). Get off there, walk back a few yards, and you're at the Gallo. The rooms are modern and comfortable, and the affiliated Ristorante Galleto is excellent. The station is within walking distance if you aren't carrying luggage and you feel like walking.
• Metropol (∗∗∗), Bahnhofplatz 3, CH-9001 St. Gallen, phone 41-71220 61 61, fax 222 08 20. Single with bath, 140-170 francs; dou-

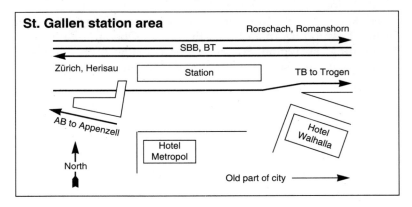

St. Gallen station area

Rorschach, Romanshorn

SBB, BT

Zürich, Herisau   Station   TB to Trogen

AB to Appenzell

North

Hotel Metropol

Hotel Walhalla

Old part of city

ble with bath, 205-230 francs. The Metropol is directly opposite the station. I have not stayed there; I have included it for its proximity to the station.

A comparison of listings in the *Swiss Hotel Guide* and maps in the Baedeker and Michelin guides yields nothing of moderate price within walking distance of the station.

RAILWAY COMPANIES IN ADDITION TO SBB
Appenzellerbahnen (AB) — meter gauge
Bodensee-Toggenburg-Bahn (BT)
Trogenerbahn (TB) — meter gauge

RECOMMENDED TRIPS
Appenzell
Konstanz, Germany
Trogen and Heiden

APPENZELL

St. Gallen	leave	0907	AB (S855, C527)
Gais	arrive	0939	
Gais	leave	0952	AB (S856, C527)
Altstätten Stadt	arrive	1013	
Altstätten Stadt	leave	1018	
Gais	arrive	1037	
Gais	leave	1040	AB (S855, C527)
Appenzell	arrive	1051	
Appenzell	leave	1058	AB (S854, C526)
Wasserauen	arrive	1109	
Wasserauen	leave	1143	
Urnäsch	arrive	1214	
Herisau	arrive	1235	
Herisau	leave	1250	BT (S870, C525)
St. Gallen	arrive	1258	

St. Gallen to Gais

Distance: 14 km
Company: Appenzellerbahnen (AB) — meter gauge
Maximum grade: 92 per mill (rack)

The AB shares with the Trogenerbahn a station in St. Gallen that is south of the west end of the SBB station. The AB line climbs out of the valley with rack assistance. The line makes several short descents, but the trend is upward, from 669 meters at St. Gallen to 916 meters at Gais. Part of the line is on private right of way, part of it runs along the side of the road, and part (not much) is street running. The carbarn is at Gais.

An Appenzellerbahnen train approaches the top of the grade up from Altstätten. The "A" (for "Anfang") on the sign indicates the beginning of the rack. Photo by J. P. Stith.

Gais to Alstätten

Distance: 8 km
Company: Appenzellerbahnen (AB) — meter gauge
Maximum grade: 160 per mill (rack)

Leaving Gais the train swings around a sharp curve, letting you see the carbarn from three sides. The line climbs briefly, then descends into the Rhine Valley with rack assistance most of the way. The ride is quite scenic. Altstätten is 200 meters lower than St. Gallen. The trains used to run on streetcar tracks to the SBB station; now there's a bus connection.

Gais to Appenzell

Distance: 6 km
Company: Appenzellerbahnen (AB) — meter gauge
Maximum grade: 63 per mill

Gais to Appenzell is a quick ride over a summit, then a sharp descent into Appenzell.

Wasserauen through Appenzell to Herisau

Distance: 27 km

Company: Appenzellerbahnen (AB) — meter gauge

Maximum grade: 37 per mill

From Appenzell the AB runs 6 kilometers southeast, climbing at about 30 per mill, to Wasserauen, where there is an aerial cable line to Ebenalp (table S2740, length, 1514 meters; ascent, 723 meters). In the other direction, the line runs west to Urnäsch, where it makes a hairpin turn, then north to Herisau. The station at Herisau is across the street from the Bodensee-Toggenburg station.

At Jakobsbad, 8 or 9 minutes from Appenzell, is an aerial cable line to Kronberg (table S2725, length, 3,223 meters; ascent, 772 meters). At Urnäsch, 4 kilometers farther, you can connect with postal buses to Schwägalp (table S854.20 in the bus volume) and the aerial cable line from Schwägalp to the summit of Säntis (table S2730, length, 2,307 meters; ascent, 1123 meters; elevation of the summit, 2,502 meters or 8,215 feet). Postal buses also connect Schwägalp with Nesslau-Neu St. Johann at the south end of the Bodensee-Toggenburg-Bahn.

The AB continues 5 kilometers beyond Herisau to Gossau, on SBB's Winterthur–St. Gallen line (table S850 and C530).

Herisau to St. Gallen

Distance: 8 km

Company: Bodensee-Toggenburg-Bahn (BT)

Maximum grade: 18 per mill (descending)

The BT is discussed at length below as part of the trip to Konstanz. Just west of St. Gallen the line crosses the Sitter River on the Sitter Viaduct, highest railway bridge in Switzerland (324 feet, 4 feet higher than Southern Pacific's Pecos River bridge near Langtry, Texas, and Burlington Northern's Crooked River bridge near Bend, Oregon).

KONSTANZ, GERMANY

St. Gallen	leave	0901	BT (S870, C525)
Romanshorn	arrive	0926	
Romanshorn	leave	0932	SBB (S820, C532)
Kreuzlingen	arrive	0957	
Kreuzlingen	leave	1012	MThB (S830, C538)
Konstanz	arrive	1015	
Konstanz	leave	1220	MThB (S830, C538)
Weinfelden	arrive	1251	
Weinfelden	leave	1308	SBB (S852)
St. Gallen	arrive	1355	

A Bodensee-Toggenburg train departs from the east end of the St. Gallen trainshed on September 13, 1983.

St. Gallen to Romanshorn

Distance: 21 km
Company: Bodensee-Toggenburg-Bahn (BT)
Maximum grade: 19 per mill

The Bodensee-Toggenburg extends from Romanshorn through St. Gallen to Nesslau-Neu St. Johann, a total of 66 kilometers. BT teams up with SBB and the Südostbahn (SOB) to offer through service between Romanshorn and Luzern.

The line from St. Gallen, where BT shares a station with SBB, passes through a short tunnel and then descends gradually through apple-growing country to the shore of the Bodensee (Lake Constance), a drop of 271 meters.

The station at Romanshorn also serves SBB's lines to Winterthur and along the shore of the Bodensee between Rorschach and Kreuzlingen. Additionally, there's an SBB ferry across the lake to Friedrichshafen, years ago the seat of the Zeppelin industry.

Romanshorn to Kreuzlingen

Distance: 19 km
Company: SBB

The line follows the shore of the Bodensee. Kreuzlingen is the junction for Konstanz, Germany, 1 kilometer away over the rails of the Mittel-Thurgau-Bahn. You could walk it. Part way there you'll be able to spot the actual border, marked by a striped pole.

In the station you can see German diesel and electric locomotives; to the east of the station is the boat dock — German Railway (Deutsche Bahn) operates an extensive boat service on the Bodensee. The town is worth exploration.

Konstanz to Weinfelden

Distance: 23 km
Company: Mittel-Thurgau-Bahn (MThB)
Maximum grade: 20 per mill

MThB trains operate from Engen, Germany, down through Singen to Konstanz, then continue to Weinfelden. The line climbs away from the lake, winding back and forth, crosses a low summit at Altishausen, then descends to Weinfelden.

From Weinfelden the MThB continues south 19 kilometers to Wil on SBB's Winterthur–St. Gallen route. There are few through trains between Konstanz and Wil. The two segments of the line are scheduled for optimal connections at their south ends rather than with each other.

Weinfelden to St. Gallen

Distance: 39 km
Company: SBB

Weinfelden–St. Gallen local trains follow the Winterthur-Romanshorn route 7 kilometers to Sulgen and join the Winterthur-St. Gallen line at Gossau, 10 km from St. Gallen. The Sulgen–Gossau line traverses an industrial area and is somewhat branchline in character. (In Switzerland this does not mean 60-pound rail, rotting wood ties, and no ballast.)

HEIDEN AND TROGEN

St. Gallen	leave	0905	1503	SBB (S880)
Rorschach	arrive	0918	1518	
Rorschach	leave	0923	1523	RHB (S857
Heiden	arrive	0943	1543	
Heiden	leave	1054	1604	bus (S857.90)
Trogen	arrive	1117	1627	
Trogen	leave	1132	1632	TB (S859)
St. Gallen	arrive	1157	1657	

St. Gallen to Rorschach

Distance: 15 km
Company: SBB
Maximum grade: 22 per mill (descending)

SBB's line from St. Gallen to Rorschach drops 271 meters in 15 kilometers, which averages out to 18 per mill (1.8 percent).

Heiden to Rorschach

Distance: 6 km
Company: Rorschach-Heiden-Bergbahn (RHB)
Maximum grade: 90 per mill (rack)

The Rorschach-Heiden-Bergbahn (RHB), opened in 1875, is one of the oldest rack-operated lines in Switzerland. In Rorschach RHB trains operate on adhesion — without rack assistance — on SBB rails from the Rorschach Hafen (Harbor) station through the main station and across the yard to connect with their own line.

The line offers fine views of the Bodensee during the ascent to Heiden, 395 meters (1,296 feet) higher than Rorschach. In good weather the trains carry open cars.

Heiden to Trogen

In Heiden, walk up the main street about a block to the square, on the far corner of which is the post office and several yellow postal buses. The suggested morning schedule hits a gap in the bus service. It provides an excuse to stop for coffee in Heiden. The bus ride to Trogen runs crossgrain to the topography and gains you another 120 meters of altitude.

Trogen to St. Gallen

Distance: 10 km
Company: Trogenerbahn (TB) — meter gauge
Maximum grade: 75 per mill

The TB was opened in 1903. It operates from a station just south of the main station in St. Gallen. The tracks pass through the station plaza and follow city streets for a way before the line becomes a side-of-the-road trolley line. The TB's operating headquarters and carbarn are at Speicher; Trogen is simply a stub-end terminal.

Trains run every 30 minutes. Trogen is a pleasant, quick turn-around excursion from St. Gallen. The village lies a little beyond the end of the rail line.

SOLOTHURN

Solothurn is 42 minutes north of Bern on the meter-gauge line of the Regionalverkehr Bern-Solothurn (ex-Solothurn-Zollikofen-Bern). It's also on the SBB line from Genève and Lausanne to Zürich via Neuchâtel and Biel, and there's hourly service to and from the Zürich airport. The main station is a busy place. RBS trains have their own platforms south of the standard gauge lines (there's a pedestrian tunnel), and the Solothurn-Niederbipp Bahn has a platform out in the open northeast of the main station building.

Solothurn straddles the Aare River and is at the base of the Jura ridge. It is an ancient walled city. The Romans called it Salodurum; the French know it as Soleure. It is a good base for exploring the Jura region, and it's within easy reach of Bern, if you want to avoid a big city and big-city hotel prices.

HOTEL
• Hotel Astoria (***), Wengistrasse, CH-4500 Solothurn, phone 41-65-22 75 71, fax 23 68 57. Single with bath, 90-105 francs; double with bath, 110-160 francs.

You don't want to walk to the Astoria from the main station with luggage. Hourly SBB locals and hourly SMB trains to and from Moutier stop at Solothurn West. Come out of the Solothurn West station, walk up the street a short block, and turn right on Wengistrasse. The hotel has a top-floor dining room which probably offers good views in nice weather. There are other restaurants nearby.

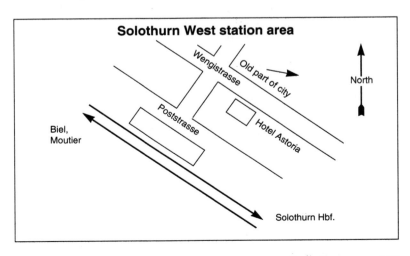

Solothurn West station area

RAILWAY COMPANIES IN ADDITION TO SBB
Emmenthal-Burgdorf-Thun (EBT)
Regionalverkehr Bern-Solothurn (RBS) — meter gauge
Solothurn-Moutier Bahn (SMB)
Solothurn-Niederbipp Bahn (SNB) — meter gauge

RECOMMENDED TRIPS
Bern, Burgdorf, and Huttwil — see the section on Bern
Glovelier, Chaux-de-Fonds, and Neuchatel
Waldenburgerbahn

BERN, BURGDORF, AND HUTTWIL
This trip is described in the section on Bern, page 63. Catch
up with it at Burgdorf or Bern.

Solothurn West	leave	0741	0841	SMB (S411)
Solothurn	arrive	0743	0843	
Solothurn	leave	0818	0849	EBT (S440)
Burgdorf	arrive	0843	0914	

Solothurn West	leave	0741	SMB (S411)
Solothurn	arrive	0743	
Solothurn	leave	0803	RBS (S420)
Bern	arrive	0840	

GLOVELIER, CHAUX-DE-FONDS, AND NEUCHATEL

Solothurn	leave	915	SMB (S411)
Solothurn West	leave	917	
Moutier	arrive	945	
Moutier	leave	949	SBB (S230, C500)
Delémont	arrive	959	
Delémont	leave	1004	SBB (S240)
Glovelier	arrive	1017	
Glovelier	leave	1019	CJ (S236)
Le Noirmont	arrive	1055	
Le Noirmont	leave	1220	CJ (S237)
Tavannes	arrive	1255	
Tavannes	leave	1300	SBB (S226)
Sonceboz-Sombeval	arrive	1307	
Sonceboz-Sombeval	leave	1350	SBB (S225, C512)
La Chaux-de-Fonds	arrive	1418	
La Chaux-de-Fonds	leave	1508	SBB (S223, C511)
Neuchâtel	arrive	1543	
Neuchâtel	leave	1606	SBB (S210, C500)
Solothurn	arrive	1645	SBB (S410, C500)

This excursion takes you up through the Jura area, well off the tourist path and into French-speaking country. The scenery is not as spectacular as the Alps, but it is beautiful — in spots, almost hauntingly so.

Solothurn to Moutier

Distance: 29 km

Company: Solothurn-Moutier (SMB)

The SMB is an outlying portion of the Emmental-Burgdorf-Thun and Vereinigte Huttwil-Bahnen system. Its red two-unit trains leave Solothurn's main station on SBB rails, cross the Aare, stop at Solothurn West, and immediately diverge onto their own line. The route climbs partway up the Jura ridge, affording good views south to the Alps, then dives into a tunnel. South of the tunnel the conductor prefaces the next station with "Nächste Halt;" north of the tunnel it's "Prochain arrêt."

Moutier to Delémont

Distance: 11 km

Company: SBB

This line is part of Swiss Federal's Basel–Lausanne route. It follows the valley of La Birse down into Delémont, where the train reverses direction to continue to Basel.

Delémont to Glovelier

Distance: 12 km

Company: SBB

Another short hop, this time on a secondary line that continues through Porrentruy and Delle to Belfort in France. You'll find the CJ train in the street behind the station at Glovelier.

Glovelier to Le Noirmont and Tavannes

Distance: 76 km

Company: Chemins de fer du Jura (CJ)

Track gauge: 1 meter

Maximum grade: 50 per mill

The Chemins de fer du Jura was put together from several railways. The first was the line from Tavannes to Tramelan, which opened in 1885. Next was a route from Saignelégier to La Chaux-de-Fonds, opened in 1902. In 1913 those two were connected by an electric railway from Le Noirmont to Tramelan. When the third line ws opened, the Tavannes–Tramelan line was electrified. All the railways in the area were brought together as the Chemins de fer du Jura in 1944, along with a standard gauge line from Porrentruy to Bonfol.

The Glovelier–Saignelégier railway was built in 1904 to standard gauge. Passenger service was replaced by buses in 1948. In 1953 the line was converted to meter gauge and electrified, and rail passenger service was restored. Of considerable help to the affairs of the CJ was the separation of the French speaking portion of Bern canton to form the canton of Jura in 1979. CJ is, so to speak, the state railway of that canton.

The train leaves Glovelier and heads into the forest. It reverses direction at Combe-Tabeillon, then climbs from 506 meters at Glovelier to 969 meters at Le Noirmont, 25 per mill most of the way. The scenery includes a gorge; there are several tunnels (which are kind of negative scenery).

If time is short, you can stay on the train to La Chaux-de-Fonds, arriving there at 1130. It's a pretty ride along ridges at about 1,000 meters elevation, then down through the streets of La Chaux-de-Fonds.

Le Noirmont is a good place to stop for lunch. From the station walk up to the main street. A few doors to your left is the Tea-Room Wenger, which is located pretty much back-to-back with the station. You could do worse than have a bowl of their soup, which does not come out of a red-and-white can, then spend a few minutes deciding among the pastries in the display case. Across the street is the Restaurant Soleil, which others in my group said was excellent, too.

From Le Noirmont the train proceeds across a ridge and down through Tramelan, where there's a carbarn.

Tavannes to La Chaux-de-Fonds
Distance: 37 km
Company: SBB

This ride is in two parts. Leaving Tavannes the train goes through a tunnel, then descends around a horseshoe curve to Sonceboz-Sombeval. There you change trains, then head southwest through a wide valley. The several lines entering La Chaux-de-Fonds all come together at various levels and drop down into the station together.

La Chaux-de-Fonds to Neuchâtel
Distance: 29 km
Company: SBB

From La Chaux-de-Fonds the train is in tunnel most of the way to Les-Hauts-Genèveys. On a good day there's a view east to the Alps and south over the Lac de Neuchâtel. The train reverses at Chambrelien before continuing to Neuchâtel. From there you can take a local or an express through Biel/Bienne to Solothurn, or go through Bern and ride the RBS up to Solothurn, or take any of several other routes, depending how much time and energy you have.

West of Neuchâtel is the Chemin de fer Touristique Vapeur

Val-de-Travers. It is open Saturdays and also on the Sundays trains operate. Getting to their museum site at St-Sulpice requires riding a train from Neuchâtel (one leaves at 9 minutes past each hour) to Fleurier (arrive at 46 past — table S221), a 2-minute connection to a postal bus (table S221.10), and a 4-minute ride to St-Sulpice (get off at the post office), then a short walk. On the second weekend of the month, May through October, the museum operates trains from Travers and Fleurier to St-Sulpice, but only the 1147 (Sunday only) and the 1440 from Travers will give you much time at the museum.

WALDENBURGERBAHN

Solothurn West	leave	927	1027	SBB (S410, C500)
Solothurn	leave	931	1031	
Oensingen	arrive	949	1049	
Oensingen	leave	1012	1102	OeBB (S412)
Balsthal	arrive	1021	1110	
Balsthal	leave	1039	1113	bus (S412.20)
Waldenburg	arrive	1103	1137	
Waldenburg	leave	1105	1147	WB (S502)
Liestal	arrive	1129	1210	
Liestal	leave	1158	1214	SBB (C510, 550)
Basel	arrive	1209	1230	
Basel	leave	1223	1323	SBB (S230, C500)
Moutier	arrive	1311	1411	
Moutier	leave	1314	1414	SMB (S411)
Solothurn West	arrive	1341	1441	
Solothurn	arrive	1343	1443	

The Waldenburgerbahn is Switzerland's only 750mm gauge railway. The excursion is described in the section on Basel, page 59. The 1012 OeBB departure from Oensingen is listed as a mixed train. There is some interesting equipment on the OeBB at Balsthal — at least there was when I was there several years ago. The place seemed a bit like a railroad museum. The equipment for the regular train that day was a former Deutsche Bundesbahn electric railcar, still in DB colors.

ZERMATT

Zermatt is a place you go not to see trains but to see the symbol of Switzerland, the Matterhorn. Probably the most touristy place in Switzerland, Zermatt is accessible only from Brig and Visp. Trains leave the narrow gauge platforms in Brig at 18 past the hour and Visp at 31 past and reach Zermatt at 42 past the next hour. Most trains leave Zermatt at 15 past the hour. They reach Visp at 30 past the next hour and Brig at 42 past (tables S140 and C576).

The line from Visp to Zermatt was surveyed in 1886. Construction began in 1889, and the line was opened in 1891. The Visp-Zermatt Railway was electrified in 1929, and in 1930 it was extended 8.5 kilometers east from Visp to a connection with the Furka-Oberalp Railway at Brig (presumably at that time it added "Brig" to its name). Soon after that the upper portion of the line was rebuilt to allow year-round operation to Zermatt.

The ride from Brig starts out westward alongside Swiss Federal Railways' line down the Rhône Valley. Your train will likely be overtaken or met by an SBB train, and you may see a Bern-Lötschberg-Simplon train on the line that climbs the north wall of the valley.

At Visp the line turns toward the south and begins climbing. Shortly out of Visp there is a picturesque stone bridge across the river to the right (west) — the best photo is looking back toward Visp (or catch it on the return trip). The valley floor ascends in steps, and the BVZ does too, with five stretches of rack operation at grades up to 125 per mill.

About midway through the first stretch of cog rail is Stalden, where the valley is deep and spanned by two high road bridges.

At Randa, about an hour from Brig, watch on the right side for the remains of a landslide that occurred in early 1991. The side of a mountain came loose and roared down into the valley right after the last train of the evening had passed. It was necessary to rebuild and relocate the railroad and the highway.

At Täsch you will see an enormous parking lot on the left. That's as far up the valley as automobiles are permitted. The BVZ runs frequent shuttle trains between Täsch and Zermatt — every 20 minutes during daylight hours.

There are no gasoline-powered automobiles in Zermatt, but the streets are crowded with battery powered taxis and trucks, bicycles, pedestrians, skiers (in season), and horse-drawn carriages. Watch your step.

HOTELS

Hotels are thick on the ground, to use a Briticism. The Swiss Hotel Guide lists 73, and there are doubtless others that are not in that book. In the station plaza is a board showing where the hotels are and a telephone so you can call for information.

I have stayed in several hotels in Zermatt. At one, well up on the world-famed list, a desk clerk told a tour group member who had broken her ankle that there were no doctors in Zermatt and she would have to be taken out by helicopter. Wrong. If you're going to break an ankle, do it in a world-famed ski resort. The cast was a work of art, with "1987" scribed into it in European-style figures.

The same hotel is memorable for complaining about how noisy the Smithsonian tour group was during dinner. The Smithsonian representative and I passed the word to the group. They were much more animated the second evening.

One year we stayed in a weird sort of place near the Gornergrat Railway station — weird meaning decor with lots of wrought iron, stained glass, and weathered wood. The bathtubs were equipped with whirlpools. One of the group used the little package of bubble bath *and* turned on the whirlpool. The result, I'm told, was worthy of *I Love Lucy*.

Two hotels remain in my mind for pleasant stays. In 1986 I stayed at the Darioli, a small, unpretentious, homey, family-run hotel on the main street. I'd stay there again. In 1995 the tour group stayed at the Hotel Julen. The accommodations, the food, and the view of the Matterhorn were wonderful. I'd stay there again too.

• Hotel Darioli (∗∗∗), Bahnhofstrasse, CH-3920 Zermatt, phone 41-28-67 27 48, fax 67 50 95. Single with bath, 75-95 francs; double with bath, 150-190 francs. It's a few minutes' walk south up the main street from the station — on the right beyond the post office.

• Romantik Hotel Julen (∗∗∗), Steinmatte, CH-3920 Zermatt, phone 41-28-67 24 81, fax 67 14 81. Single with bath, 126 francs; double with bath, 250-284 francs (dinner is included). Head up the main street to the marmot fountain, turn left down the hill and across the brook and the river; it's at the second cross street. It's 10 minutes if your luggage doesn't hold you back. An easier river-level route requires a look at the map of Zermatt posted at the station.

The hotel rates shown are for midsummer. Prices are lower in fall and late spring and higher for the skiing season, early February to early April.

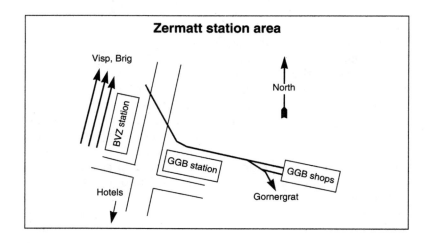

Zermatt station area

RESTAURANTS

If you're staying at a hotel garni — no restaurant — you'll have to search for dinner. In 1986 the group happened on Chez Gaby, run by a retired boxer, going by the pictures on the wall. He does the cooking as you watch, and the food comes off the heat and onto your plate about as fast as he can turn around. To get there, go up the main street to the marmot fountain, turn left, then down to the brook and turn right. I hope Gaby is still in business.

GORNERGRAT

Zermatt	leave	1000	GGB (S142, C578)
Riffelalp	arrive	1019	
Gornergrat	arrive	1043	
Gornergrat	leave	1107	
Riffelalp	arrive	1132	
Zermatt	arrive	1151	

Distance: 9 km
Company: Gornergrat-Bahn (GGB) — meter gauge
Maximum grade: 200 per mill (rack)

Go to the station, across the street from the BVZ station, buy your ticket (the Swiss Pass gives you a discount), and join the line waiting for the next train. Trains leave Zermatt every 24 minutes, except during May and November, when schedules are reduced to about hourly.

Trains often run in two or more sections. A green-and-white disk on the front of the car indicates another section following.

Construction of the GGB began in 1896. All the curves were laid to a uniform radius of 80 meters (36 inches in HO scale) and

Gornergrat-Bahn single car 3018 stands at the Gornergrat station on March 10, 1993. The castle-like building also houses a post office. In the background is the Matterhorn, which is practically an icon of Switzerland.

most of the line has a uniform grade. The line opened in late 1898 and year-round service began in 1929. The GGB was electrified from the beginning. Cars operate on three-phase current, which requires two overhead wires.

Not far out of Zermatt you start getting good views of the Matterhorn (the right side of the car offers the better view). At the summit are a hotel and restaurant, a gift shop, and a post office.

From the station at Riffelalp it's about a 10-minute walk up a path behind the station building, then to the left and across the tracks to a meadow where you can get photos of trains on double track with the Matterhorn as a backdrop (like the cover photo). Footpaths in the area also lead to the Berghotel Riffelalp, whose sunny terrace is a good place for lunch.

ZÜRICH

Zürich is the largest city in Switzerland and the center of its rail system. It's also the location of the country's principal international airport. If you make Zürich your last stop, you can spend a final day shopping for souvenirs and riding suburban trains and streetcars, or you can go back to almost anywhere for another try at good weather or for a second look. Luzern, Mount Rigi, St. Gallen, and Bern are all about an hour away.

There are two model railroad shops in the area east of the Limmat River. One is on Marktgasse just east of the Rathaus Bridge (two bridges upstream from the station); the other is directly across the river from the station and one or two streets back from the river. The Franz Karl Weber toy store (part of a nationwide chain) on the east side of Bahnhofstrasse is also a good source of model railroad equipment.

HOTELS

• Glockenhof (****), Sihlstrasse 31, CH-8023 Zürich 1, phone 41-1-211 56 50, fax 41-1-211 56 60. Single with bath, 170-240 francs; double with bath, 250-350 francs.

I have stayed at the Glockenhof several times. Take a streetcar from the Hauptbahnhof down Bahnhofstrasse toward the lake (I think routes 6, 7, 11, and 13 cover that route.) Get off at Füsslistrasse, the second stop on Bahnhofstrasse. Walk west

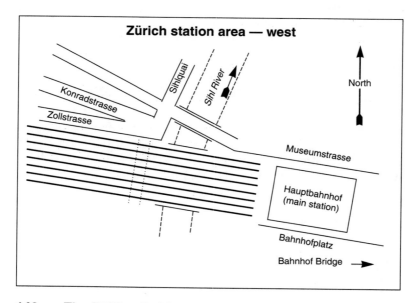

Zürich station area — west

(right) a short block and you should be there. A map is helpful — there are odd angles in the streets west of Bahnhofstrasse.

• Montana (∗∗∗), Konradstrasse 39, CH-8005 Zürich, phone 41-1-271 69 00, fax 272 30 70. Single with bath 160-210 francs; double with bath, 225-290 francs.

The Montana is northwest of the Hauptbahnhof. Instead of walking all the way into the station, use the concourse under the tracks about halfway out the platform, walk toward the high-numbered tracks and out the end, and Konradstrasse will be diagonally to your left. I have not stayed at the Montana; I've chosen it for it proximity to the station combined with lower rates than you find out the south side of the station.

• Limmathof (∗∗), Limmatquai 142, CH-8023 Zürich, phone 41-1-261 42 20, fax 262 02 17. Single with bath, 95-125 francs; double with bath, 125-165 francs. The Limmathof is across the river from the Hauptbahnhof, a door or two away from the lower terminal of the Polybahn funicular. It was clean, comfortable, and convenient in 1986.

HOTELS NEAR ZÜRICH

• Hotel Terminus (∗∗∗), Bahnhofplatz 1, CH-5200 Brugg, phone 41-56-441 18 21, fax 441 82 20. Single with bath, 95-110 francs; double with bath, 155-170 francs.

Brugg is about 25 minutes by fast train toward Basel. The hotel is directly across from the station, and the northerly subway under the platforms may be the easiest way to cross the street. The proprietor, Alfred Lang, is a railfan. In the attic of the hotel is a large model railroad that cheerfully combines O and No. 1 gauges and scale and tinplate. It is open to view one

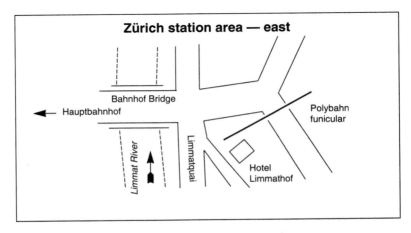

evening a week and sometimes by request. The affiliated Orient Express Restaurant is superb.

• Seehotel Meierhof (∗∗∗∗), Bahnhofstrasse 4, CH-8810 Horgen, phone 41-1-725 29 61, fax 725 55 23. Single with bath, 95-200 francs; double with bath, 200-260 francs.

Horgen is 19 to 23 minutes by train from Zürich Hauptbahnhof on the line to Pfäffikon, Ziegelbrücke, and Chur (tables S720 and S1700-S8). There is a Horgen Oberdorf station on the line to Zug and Luzern, but there's an implication in "Oberdorf" of a walk down to lake level. Readers have recommended the Meierhof for its views of the tracks and the lake. I would expect the rooms with lake views cost more than rooms with track views.

• Thalwilerhof (∗∗), Bahnhofstrasse 16, CH 8800 Thalwil, phone 41-1-720 06 03, fax 722 29 77. Single with bath, 72-98 francs; without bath, 63-72 francs; double with bath, 115-160 francs; without bath, 95-105 francs.

Thalwil is 11 to 15 minutes from Zurich Hauptbahnhof. It is where the lines to Luzern and Chur part company; many long-distance trains stop there as well as suburban trains. I have chosen the Thalwilerhof simply from its listing in the Swiss Hotel Guide — it looks like a convenient and inexpensive place to stay.

RESTAURANTS

The Bahnhofbuffet in the Hauptbahnhof consists of ten different restaurants covering all price ranges. They have a good reputation. Years ago a friend recommended the Zeughauskeller at Bahnhofstrasse 28a (Paradeplatz). You stand in line until places clear, then you sit at long tables while waiters bring you hearty food and drink. It's noisy and busy, and I eat there on most of my visits to Zürich. The Pusztawurst, a Hungarian sausage (I think it's No. 62 on the menu) is real good.

HAUPTBAHNHOF (MAIN STATION)

The Hauptbahnhof is a scene of intense activity. On the main level are 16 tracks numbered 3 to 18 from south to north. Underneath the station is a shopping area with everything an American mall has except anchoring department stores and acres of parking — plus a laundromat. Under the shopping area at the south end are tracks 1 and 2, for the Sihltal-Zürich-Uetliberg-Bahn. Under the north end are tracks 21-24 for suburban trains that run through the tunnel under the Limmat River.

The station hosts exotic equipment: German ICEs, Spanish Talgos, and Italian Pendolinos. Midevening several sleeper

It is nearly departure time from Zürich on September 14, 1983. The starting signal indicates "brakes okay."

trains depart — worth strolling along the platforms to see.

It may help your sense of direction to know that the train-shed opens to the west-northwest, and the Sihl River flows north under the trainshed about halfway out along the platforms and shortly joins the Limmat, which flows north out of the lake.

OTHER STATIONS

Several other stations in Zürich are served by local trains; most long-distance trains roar right through.

• Enge, on the lines to Luzern, Gotthard, and Chur, is on streetcar lines 5, 6, 7, and 13 almost due south of Hauptbahnhof.

• Oerlikon, on the lines to St. Gallen, Schaffhausen, and the airport, is in the northern part of the the city on streetcar lines 10 and 11. At Oerlikon the catenary wires are hung from bridges that span the right of way — no poles to get in the way of your photos.

• Stadelhofen, on suburban routes to Rapperswil and Winterthur, is a couple of blocks east of the Limmat where it flows out of the lake. It is served by streetcar lines 11 and 15 and the Forchbahn.

• Wollishofen is out beyond Enge.

• Wiedikon is between Enge and Hauptbahnhof.

• Hardbrücke is at the junction of the line to Oerlikon and the line to Baden and Brugg.

• Altstetten is out beyond Hardbrücke on the line to Baden and Brugg.

STREETCARS

Zürich has an extensive streetcar system. An all-day pass is available for 5 francs, and the Swiss Pass is valid. In the absence of any other plan, a good way to see the system might be to board a car, ride to the end of the line, ride back, then take another. You will find maps at each stop.

Lines 7 and 9 have a stretch of tunnel running in the eastern part of the city. The three stations in the tunnel have center platforms, so the cars run on the left-hand track. At the west end of the tunnel the tracks enter separately, with the inbound track ducking under the outbound. At the east portal, west of the Schwamendinger Platz stop, the two tracks cross at grade.

The Zürich Tram Museum is worth a visit. It is at the Wartau stop on Line 13 in Höngg, open Wednesday evenings from 1930 to 2100. On the first Saturday of the month the museum's cars operate to the museum from the Bahnhofquai stop at the Hauptbahnhof, on the hour from 1400 to 1700. For information, write to the Verein Tram-Museum, Postfach, CH-8023 Zürich.

STREETCAR RESTAURANT

From May through October the ChuChiChästli tram restaurant operates from the Bellevue Plaza stop (take Line 4 from the Hauptbahnhof), down where the lake flows into the Limmat.

During the course (or courses) of a 2-hour dinner, the tram makes four different 25-minute loops around downtown Zürich. For information and reservations, call 41-77-63 35 05.

RECOMMENDED TRIPS
Bremgarten-Dietikon
Forchbahn
Rapperswil
Uetliberg
Zürich Flughafen (Airport)

BREMGARTEN-DIETIKON

Zürich	leave	0913		SBB (S710)
Dietikon	arrive	0927		
Dietikon	leave	0933		BD (S654)
Wohlen	arrive	1008		

Dietikon to Wohlen

Distance: 19 km
Company: Bremgarten-Dietikon (BD) — meter gauge
Maximum grade: 50 per mill

The Bremgarten-Dietikon is rather a surprise so close to Zürich — a meter gauge line with sharp curves and steep grades. The line climbs from Dietikon at 388 meters over a summit at 550 meters and drops to Bremgarten, 390 meters. As the train crosses the River Reuss at Bremgarten you can get a good photo of the adjacent covered road bridge. The line climbs over another summer of 453 meters, then descends to Wohlen at 423 meters.

On from Wohlen

North

Wohlen	leave	1012	1045	SBB (S653)
Lenzburg	arrive	1022	1055	
Lenzburg	leave		1103	SBB (S641)
Rupperswill	arrive		1106	

Back to Zürich

Lenzburg	leave	1033	1102	SBB S650)
Zurich	arrive	1054	1122	

South

Wohlen	leave	1115		SBB (S653)
Rotkreuz	arrive	1141		
Zug	arrive	1155		
Rotkreuz	leave	1150		SBB (S660)
Luzern	arrive	1207		
Rotkreuz	leave	1150		SBB (S600)
Arth-Goldau	arrive	1205		

The line through Wohlen from Lenzburg to Rotkreuz and Arth-Goldau is part of the main north-south freight route through Switzerland.

One stop west of Lenzburg is Rupperswil, a good train-watching spot. All trains between Zürich and the west and some Zürich–Basel trains pass through at speed. The line is four tracks wide and there are no intervening catenary masts. For photography, the westbound platform is better, and morning to mid-afternoon is the best light.

Trains run southeast from Wohlen at 15 past each hour to Rotkreuz and Zug. From Rotkreuz you can get local trains to Luzern and to Arth-Goldau. Zug is a busy junction where the line from Zürich splits for Luzern and the Gotthard Route.

FORCHBAHN

The Forchbahn is a meter gauge suburban line that operates from the plaza in front of the Stadelhofen station. Trains start out on the rails of streetcar line 11, run through Zumikon in a subway, then take to the side of the road for the rest of the run to Esslingen. Trains run every 15 minutes to Forch, where the shops are located. Half terminate there; half continue.

The 17-kilometer ride from Stadelhofen to Esslingen takes 36 minutes. The line climbs over a mountain and offers occasional good views of mountains in the distance. Postal buses run from Esslingen to SBB stations at Uster every half hour and at Stäfa and Uerikon every hour. Or you can simply take the next Forchbahn train back to Zürich.

RAPPERSWIL

Take a suburban train southeast through Zürich's Gold Coast, the east shore of the Zürichsee (table S730, S-Bahn line S7). Trains leave the Hauptbahnhof (lower level, north end) at 12 and 42 minutes past each hour and take 44 minutes to Rapperswil. Among your choices for the return to Zürich are:
• Cross the lake to Pfäffikon and ride back to Zürich along the west shore of the lake.
• Continue in the same general direction to Ziegelbrücke and pick up that same route.
• Ride through Rüti to Oerlikon, Effretikon, or Winterthur, then to Zürich. If you take the line to Winterthur (table S754), at Bauma watch for the trains of the Dampfbahn-Verein Zürcher Oberland (Zurich Upland Steam Railway Association). They operate on the first and third Sunday of the month, May through October (table S742).

UETLIBERG

Distance: 9 km
Company: Sihltal-Zürich-Uetliberg-Bahn (SZU)
Maximum grade: 70 per mill

The Uetliberg is a mountain southwest of the heart of Zürich, on the west shore of the Zürichsee. A ride up is a nice way to spend part of a sunny afternoon. The altitude of the summit station is 813 meters, twice the altitude of Zürich Hauptbahnhof.

SZU trains depart from track 2 of the Hauptbahnhof, down under the shopping area, at 7 and 37 minutes past each hour (table S713). The trains take 23 minutes to climb through a residential area, then through woods to the summit station. From there it is a pleasant walk on a paved path to the summit, where you'll find a restaurant, an observation tower, and good views. Trains leave for Zürich at 8 and 38 past.

Note that Uetliberg trains use an offset trolley wire. They share track but not voltage with SZU's trains to Sihlbrugg (table S712). Uetliberg cars use pantographs offset to one side and are painted orange with a red stripe. Sihltalbahn cars have centered pans and are red with an orange stripe.

ZÜRICH FLUGHAFEN (AIRPORT)

This is, unfortunately, a necessary trip, unless you manage to wangle a residency permit. The rail line through the Zürich airport was opened on April 29, 1980, by Queen Elizabeth II of England. She rode on the first long-distance train from the airport (the plaque in the station doesn't say where she went).

The 10-minute, 9-kilometer ride from the Hauptbahnhof to the airport is unscenic and something of an anticlimax after two weeks of the Glacier Express and Bernina Pass and the Jungfrau, but it's easier than the trip to most American airports.

Trains leave the Hauptbahnhof five times each hour. Look for the airplane symbol on the train departure boards.

ODDS AND ENDS

That, honey, is probably an end. — GEORGE BOOTH CARTOON CAPTION

This section holds items that are too small to merit their own chapter or resisted classification.

Romont

While riding from Lausanne to Bern my eye was caught by the walled city of Romont, about 40 km from Lausanne and 57 km from Bern. I've earmarked it for exploration next chance I get. It's also the junction with the Gruyère-Fribourg-Morat standard gauge line to Bulle (Table 254) — GFM also has meter gauge lines in the area.

Olten

Olten is a busy place. The Lausanne–Bern–Zürich and Genève–Neuchatel–Zürich lines converge just west of the station, then join the Basel–Luzern line through the station. If you want to spend an hour sitting on a bench on a platform and simply watching trains, that's the place. On the south wall of the trainshed of the Olten station is the zero kilometer marker. All rail distances in Switzerland are measured from there. Just west of the station a castle and a church overlook the Aare River. With a little walking you could probably find a good photo angle.

Freight route

Freight traffic moving between Basel and the Gotthard Route at Arth-Goldau travels through Frick, Brugg, Lenzburg, and Rotkreuz — timetable routes 700, 652, and 653. It avoids the congestion of Olten and the necessity and impossibility of reversing at Luzern. Between Rotkreuz and Arth-Goldau the route follows the west shore of the Zugersee (Lake Zug). You can see the line, even if you're too far away to take down engine numbers, from the summit of Mount Rigi. The station buffet at Arth-Goldau has open-air tables that offer a closer view of the trains on that line. If you position yourself right, you can keep an eye on trains on the Zürich side of the station, too.

Model railroad show

The Swiss model railroad industry has its annual show in the Transport Museum in Luzern during the first or second week of October. It is open to the public.

INDEX

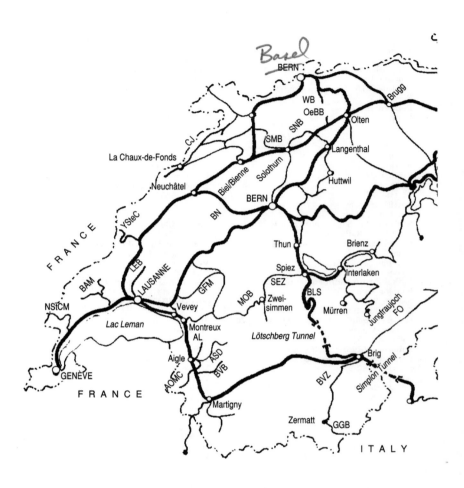

Not to scale. Not all rail lines are shown.

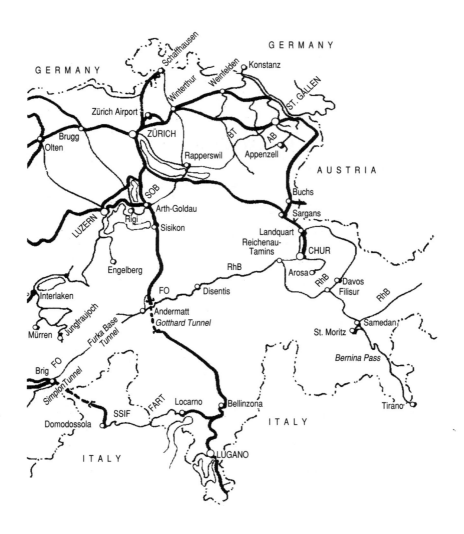

Railway map of Switzerland   159

Other guidebooks in this series are:

The Railfan Guide to Austria   **$17.95**
The Reluctant Railfan's Introduction to Europe   **$17.95**

Available where you bought this book, or order direct from:

George H. Drury
4139 West McKinley Court
Milwaukee, Wisconsin 53208-2765
Phone and fax: 414-344-7747
E-mail: GeorgDrury@aol.com

Shipping: $3.05 for the first book ordered;
$1.05 for each additional book ordered at the same time.

Wisconsin residents please add applicable sales tax.

Books in preparation:

The Railfan Guide to Germany
The Railfan Guide to Britain and Ireland

Watch for advertisements in *Trains* and
International Railway Traveler